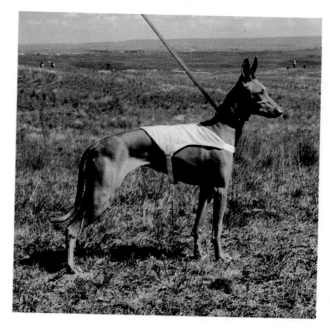

PHARAOH HOUNDS
KW-182

Photography: Isabelle Francais, Mary McCormack, Kathleen O'Brien, Phillip M. Qualls, Ron Reagan, Sue M. Sefscik, Vincent Serbin, and Sally Anne Thompson.

Drawings: Scott Boldt, Richard Crammer, Richard Davis, Andrew Prendimano, John R. Quinn, and Alexandra Suchenko.

Title page: *The Pharaoh Hound can trace its lineage back to about 3000 BC in the land of Egypt. It is believed that the legendary King Tutankhamen was an admirer of these dogs. Owner, Paul L. Hooper, Jr.*

The text of this book represents the combined efforts of the author and the editorial staff of T.F.H. Publications, Inc., which is the originator of all sections of the book except the chapters dealing with the breed history, breed description, versatility and grooming. Additionally, the portrayal of canine pet products in this book is for general instructive value only; the appearance of such products does not necessarily constitute an endorsement by the author, the publisher, or the owners of the dogs portrayed in this book.

Distributed in the UNITED STATES by T.F.H. Publications, Inc., One T.F.H. Plaza, Neptune City, NJ 07753; in CANADA to the Pet Trade by H & L Pet Supplies Inc., 27 Kingston Crescent, Kitchener, Ontario N2B 2T6; Rolf C. Hagen Ltd., 3225 Sartelon Street, Montreal 382 Quebec; in CANADA to the Book Trade by Macmillan of Canada (A Division of Canada Publishing Corporation), 164 Commander Boulevard, Agincourt, Ontario M1S 3C7; in ENGLAND by T.F.H. Publications Limited, Cliveden House/Priors Way/Bray, Maidenhead, Berkshire SL6 2HP, England; in AUSTRALIA AND THE SOUTH PACIFIC by T.F.H. (Australia) Pty. Ltd., Box 149, Brookvale 2100 N.S.W., Australia; in NEW ZEALAND by Ross Haines & Son, Ltd., 82 D Elizabeth Knox Place, Panmure, Auckland, New Zealand; in the PHILIPPINES by Bio-Research, 5 Lippay Street, San Lorenzo Village, Makati Rizal; in SOUTH AFRICA by Multipet Pty. Ltd., Box 235 New Germany, South Africa 3620. Published by T.F.H. Publications, Inc. Manufactured in the United States of America by T.F.H. Publications, Inc.

PHARAOH HOUNDS

Sue M. Sefscik

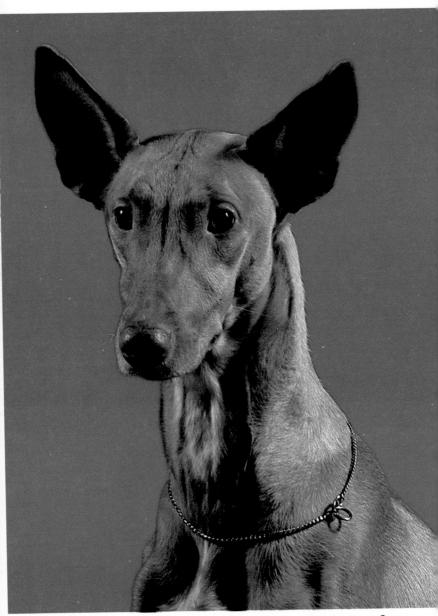

The Pharaoh Hound has the ability to hunt by sight as well as by scent. Owner, Paul L. Hooper, Jr.

Contents

HISTORY OF THE
PHARAOH HOUND...............................6

DESCRIPTION OF THE BREED......... 14
Standard for the Breed

GROOMING THE
PHARAOH HOUND........................... 24
A Step-by-Step Grooming Procedure

VERSATILITY OF THE BREED...........29

SELECTING YOUR DOG....................33
Where to Buy; Pet or Show Dog; Male or Female; Adult or Pup; What to Look for in a Puppy; Pedigree and Registration

THE NEW FAMILY MEMBER.............49
Advance Preparation; Finding a Veterinarian; Children and Puppies; Be a Good Neighbor; Getting Acquainted

FEEDING REQUIREMENTS............... 59
The Puppy's Meals; Comparison Shopping; Developing Good Eating Habits; Feeding Guidelines

ACCOMMODATIONS............................69
The Dog Bed; The Crate; The Dog House; Cleanliness; Exercise; Exercising for You and Your Dog; Nylon Discs; Polyurethane Flexible Floppy Flying Discs; Tug Toys; Balls

HOUSEBREAKING AND
TRAINING 87
Housebreaking; Patience, Persistence, and Praise; Training; When and How to Train; The Collar and Leash; Giving Commands; Some Specific Commands

BEHAVIOR MODIFICATION..............101
Problems with the Barking Dog; Aggressive Behavior and Dominance; Destructive Tendencies

HEALTH CARE................................112
Swallowing Foreign Objects; What Toys Are Safe for Dogs?; If Your Pet Swallows Poison; Danger in the Home; Vehicle Travel Safety; Protect Yourself First; Administering Medicine; In Case of an Accident; Protecting Your Pet; Inoculations; Distemper; Canine Hepatitis; Leptospirosis; Rabies; Parvovirus; Lyme Disease; Parainfluenza; External Parasites; Internal Parasites; Canine Senior Citizens

PREVENTIVE DENTAL CARE..........138
All Dogs Need to Chew; Natural Chew Bones; Rawhide Chews; Nylon Chew Devices; Floss or Loss; The Importance of Prevention; Canine Dental Breakthrough

BREEDING......................................153
The Female "In Season"; When to Breed; Choosing the Stud; Preparation for Breeding; The Female in Whelp; Preparing for the Puppies; Whelping; Raising the Puppies; Weaning the Puppies; The Decision to Spay or Neuter

DOGS AND THE LAW..................... 172
Dogs as Property; General Guidelines for Dog Owners; Travel; Cruelty; Landlords and Dogs

INDEX...190

REQUIRED READING......................192

History of the Pharaoh Hound

The Pharaoh Hound is believed to have descended from the dogs pictured on the Egyptian kings' tombs, which explains how he got his name. Pictures on ancient Egyptian buildings show that the Pharaoh Hounds were used by the pharaohs to hunt rabbits, ostriches, and other wild game found in Egypt from 3000 to 2000 BC.

Pharaoh fanciers also believe that these dogs were the supposed god heretofore known as "Anubis," the Jackal God, to the ancients. Anubis, the Egyptian god of the dead, is pictured as a man with a canine-like head. He is found on temple walls; he is sculpted into artworks. Up until recently, it was believed that the Egyptians worshiped a jackal. However, no jackals have ever been found in that ancient land. Therefore, it would seem prudent to revise this legend and call "Anubis" the Pharaoh Hound God instead.

Evidence that the Pharaoh Hound was the preferred Egyptian dog is found in this translation, "The red long-tailed dog goes at night into the stalls of the hills; he is better than the long-faced dog." Additionally, in 1935, a tomb was found in a cemetery west of the pyramid of Cheops at Giza. This tomb belonged to a dog named Abuwtiyuw; from the inscriptions

This Pharaoh Hound puppy exhibits the remarkable alertness that is characteristic of its breed. Owner, Sue M. Sefscik.

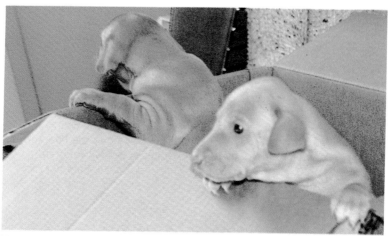

Not unlike pups of many other breeds, Pharaoh Hound youngsters are eager to explore their surroundings. Owner, Sue M. Sefscik.

on the tomb, this burial was carried out with all the usual trappings of royal burials at that time.

A drawing was found on the tomb of Antefa II, dated circa 2300 BC. It shows how much today's Pharaoh Hound resembles the ancient hounds of Egypt: the ears are the same; the tail is still generally the same; and the feet are catlike—rather than heavily sitting on his feet, the Pharaoh poises on his pads. In addition, the Pharaoh Hound often reposes into what is called the "Anubis position." This pose is shown in many ancient Egyptian drawings and is similar to the position of the Sphinx.

It is believed that the Phoenicians, one of the major seagoing peoples of the ancient world, carried the Pharaoh Hounds in their ships across the Mediterranean from Egypt. The Phoenicians' trading network extended throughout the Mediterranean. They established colonies in North Africa, Spain, Ibiza, Sicily, and Malta. The Phoenicians, as astute traders, realized the value of excellent exotic hunting dogs to peoples throughout the ancient world, which made the Pharaoh Hound a valuable trade item and companion for the Phoenician colonists.

It is likely that the Phoenicians deposited Pharaohs on many islands. If breeding took place in relative isolation, the Pharaoh would have bred true. The Phoenicians placed Pharaohs on Ibiza; there they interbred with

The Pharaoh Hound is a very energetic breed of dog. Be sure to provide your Pharaoh with regular exercise to keep him in tiptop physical condition.

more white-colored dogs and evolved into the Ibizan Hound. The Phoenicians also deposited Pharaohs in Sicily; there they bred truer than on Ibiza, and, today a breed known as "Cirneco dell'Etna" exists which is close to the Pharaoh Hound in type. Finally, on the islands of Malta, Gozo and Luzo evolved today's Pharaoh Hound.

It is not unusual to visit Malta and never see a Pharaoh; they are usually placed on the rooftops as guard dogs. In addition, they are used for hunting rabbits for food and sport. In the rocks of Malta, hunters place nets along an opening in the rocks, and the Pharaohs bark and chase and flush the rabbit out into the net.

In Malta, the Pharaoh is known as "Kelb Tal Fenek," which literally translated means "dog of the rabbit," based no doubt on the breed's rabbit hunting abilities. In Malta, through selective breeding, farmers have kept only the best and most avid hunters. All others were put down for the past two or three thousand years, resulting in a breed of dog whose face literally glows when allowed to pursue a related activity such as lure-coursing.

The training of these hounds is handed down from generation to generation. At one time, only the best hunters were kept; usually, these were the females. With the growing popularity of the breed, however, whole litters are now kept and nurtured to full growth. The Maltese have made Tal

During the course of their trading expeditions, Phoenicians left Pharaoh Hounds throughout the Mediterranean area. On the island of Ibiza, these dogs were bred with more white-colored dogs and thereby evolved this dog: the Ibizan Hound. Owner, Kathleen O'Brien.

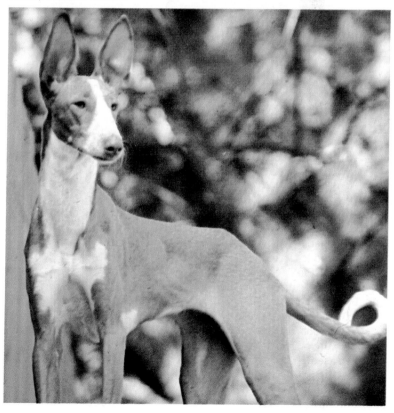

History of the Pharaoh Hound

The Pharaoh Hound has large upright ears that are carried erect when alert. The chiseled, elegant head rests upon a long, slightly arched neck. The body is lithe with an almost straight topline.

Fenek their national dog and realize they have a national treasure to share with the rest of the world.

Since the Pharaoh is a sighthound, it is more difficult to train him to hunt during the daytime. There are many distractions for him to see; therefore, most of the hunting on Malta is done at night, when there is less to divert his attention. Usually, four or five men will meet sometime after midnight, all with their dogs on leads. Once a scent is found, the hounds are set free, with the men following their dogs. Remember, the ground is rocky and treacherous on Malta and its accompanying islands, and there is not always a full moon and it is often hard to see at night.

The hunt on Malta runs something like this: once the hounds have marked the scent to ground, they will set up a constant barking until their masters reach that spot. The dogs are then placed back on their leads. Nets are placed over the rocks where the rabbit could escape. A ferret is then let loose; he wears a collar with a bell. One hound is permitted to follow the ferret's movement by listening to the bell. Being natural hunters, Pharaohs take to this final chase with eager anticipation, usually jumping upon the walls of rocks

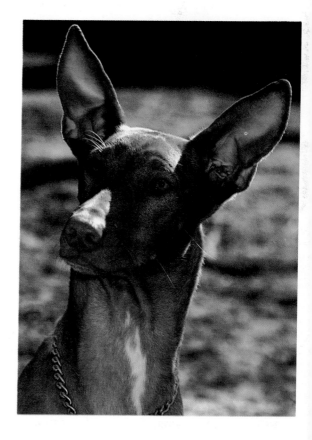

The Pharaoh Hound's large ears and amber-colored eyes lend to the breed's unique appearance.

so they can view all bolts the rabbit may make.

When the rabbit bolts (and if there is no net to stop him), the hound catches and frequently kills the rabbit. If the net stops him, the rabbit is subsequently killed by the hunter. The rabbit is then skinned and ready for the pot!

The skin can be saved and is occasionally used for training a "teenage" Pharaoh Hound to hunt. He is placed with the skin in an enclosed yard and is allowed to pounce on the skin and "kill" it; this makes him familiar with the scent and his job for the future, the actual hunting process.

Pharaoh Hounds were imported to England in the early 1930s, but disappeared again until 1963 when Major General Block and his wife, Pauline, imported a male. Block had been stationed in Malta and his wife became fascinated with the breed. While stationed in Malta, many English friends visited the Blocks, and they too became interested in the breed. Various females and males were imported to England and thus started the English line of Pharaoh Hounds.

In July 1967, the first Pharaoh Hound arrived in the United States. "Fqira" was imported by Ruth Taft Hobbs Harper, an American Kennel Club judge. Mrs. Harper first saw the Pharaoh in the *Dog World Annual* from England; thereafter, she began making inquiries about importing a bitch from England. Fqira was later registered by the Pharaoh Hound Club of America as PHCA #000001.

The only hounds directly imported to the United States from Malta were three imported around 1976 by W. Valerie Rees of Val-Ed's House of Pharaohs. While in English quarantine, all three contracted parvovirus, an unknown and relatively new disease at that time. One male subsequently died; the other male and female survived. The female, Ch. Val-Ed's Strickland Tifla, F.Ch., became a foundation for Mrs. Rees's kennel. Tifla was the top producing Pharaoh bitch in the United States, and in 1987 was the American Kennel Club's top producing bitch for all breeds.

The breed is slowly becoming popular in the United States. The Pharaoh Hound Club of America (PHCA) was established in 1970, and in 1983 the American Kennel Club (AKC) recognized the breed. The breed was first allowed full participation in AKC events as a member of the Hound Group on January 1, 1984.

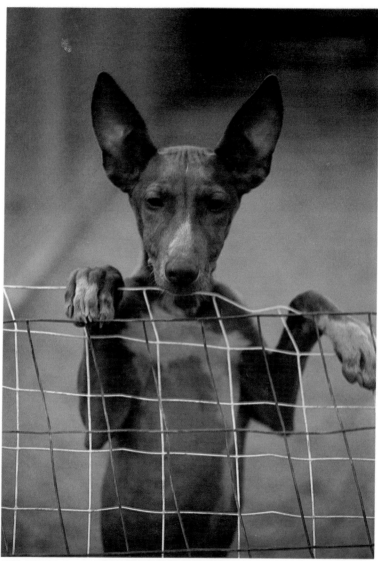

With strangers, the Pharaoh Hound is wary but not aggressive; with members of his human family, he is warm and affectionate.

Description of the Breed

The Pharaoh Hound is a medium-sized dog, with adult males not normally exceeding 25 inches in height at the shoulder and about 60 pounds in weight. A female will normally not exceed 24 inches and about 50 pounds.

Pharaohs are shorthaired dogs and are colored mostly red with white markings. The white markings are a distinct characteristic of the breed.

Remembering how the Maltese people still use the Pharaoh to hunt at night by the light of the moon, it is imperative to the breed that these white markings remain on the dogs. In my opinion, if breeders fail to retain the unique white markings of the Pharaoh Hound, then what is left is a Viszla with prick ears! The white markings are an integral part of being a Pharaoh, and the all-red (with no white markings)

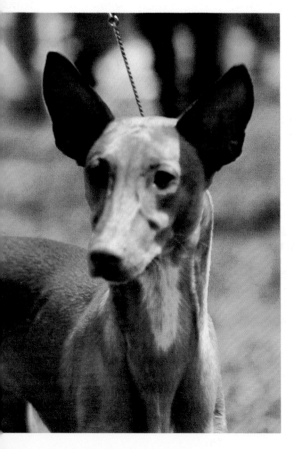

Lovely head study of a Pharaoh Hound. This is Ch. Val-Ed's Dija Tal Red Rose, C.D., owned by Sue M. Sefscik.

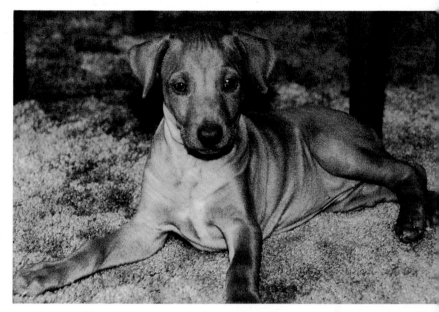

Your new Pharaoh Hound puppy will need some time to adjust to his new home. Be patient with him and you will be rewarded with his loyalty and affectionate companionship.

dog is not a true representative of the breed.

White markings are found on the head, chest, toes and are preferred on the tip of the tail. White on the sides, back or shoulders is a disqualification to showing the dog. Dogs with white on the back or sides are called "mismarked." They are not allowed to be shown at an AKC event or to be coursed at an ASFA trial. White flecking on the muzzle is also undesirable.

The ears should be upright and pricked and the tail carried well curved over the body when in motion. The eyes should almost blend into the color of the coat; they should never be blue or yellow. As with other breeds, proper bite, full dentition, and nearly single tracking are also desired.

Pharaoh Hounds are sighthounds; however, they do not have the "usual" sighthound temperament. Most people think of sighthounds as aloof, dignified and stand-offish. However, I feel that Pharaohs do not actually fit this description. They may look regal and royal while reclining in their usual Anubis position, but once a person gets to know the "real dog" behind the regality, a friendly, happy-go-lucky pal is usually found.

A Pharaoh is similar to the other sighthounds in his hunting ability. However, the Pharaoh hunts by both sight and scent, unlike any of the other sighthounds except his closest relative, the Ibizan. Like the Ibizan, the Pharaoh will also bark when chasing a lure. The Pharaoh can see from greater distances than most other breeds—this is why Pharaohs are classified as sighthounds. However, a Pharaoh also hunts by scent, much like a Beagle or Basset.

Pharaohs use their sense of scent more to hunt than most other sighthounds. They seem to explore things with their noses as well as with their eyes, and in addition, have a very keen sense of hearing.

The Pharaoh has been known to pursue his game over long distances, usually disregarding his panic-stricken owner calling vainly after him. Once game is spotted and the chase begins, all calls and commands will be in vain because of the Pharaoh's

Pharaoh Hounds are renowned and respected for their abilities in lure coursing.

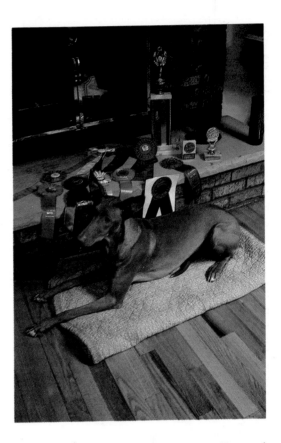

With his intelligence, outgoing personality, and even disposition, the Pharaoh Hound can be a good candidate for dog show competition.

deep-rooted hunting instinct. Obviously, a remedy to this situation is to keep the Pharaoh on a lead at all times, only letting him run loose in a securely enclosed area. Many Pharaohs are great escape artists, so a fence must be well maintained to keep a Pharaoh from jumping over or through it. Many Pharaohs are also great diggers and have been known to make their way under a fence, given due opportunity.

Pharaoh Hounds are also known for two characteristics distinct to the breed: smiling and blushing. Many Pharaohs, when greeting a person they have met before or when their owners come home from work, will crinkle up their noses, pull back their lips from their teeth and actually smile, much the same way as humans. Sometimes, if they smile too long and get very excited, they will sneeze several times. The sneezing brings down fluids to lubricate the lips so they don't become stuck. However, some people might interpret this as a snarl, since it is very

Description of the Breed

unusual looking and most people aren't used to the smiling, Cheshire cat grin!

Blushing is unique to Pharaohs; according to *Ripley's Believe It or Not*, they are the only mammal known to blush other than humans. They blush when excited or happy. In these dogs, their ears turn a bright flush red and usually the blush travels down to their pink noses, making them a "hot pink."

Pharaohs should be friendly; they gently sniff and investigate strangers' and friends' eyes, noses and usually armpits, which brings embarrassment to some

The Pharaoh Hound is a piece of living history, as he looks like his ancestors of some several thousand years ago. In the dog fancy, retaining purity of type is known as breeding true.

This little tyke is all tuckered out after a hard day of play. Your Pharaoh Hound pup will appreciate the opportunity to snooze in a nice quiet spot all his own.

people and laughter to others.

Pharaohs do not usually kennel well; they need a lot of attention and personal affection. A large, impersonal kennel situation does not permit the Pharaoh to establish his outgoing temperament. The friendly Pharaoh is much easier to live with, and most people consider their dogs as "pets" first and "show dogs" second.

As for the Pharaoh and children, with the normal, outgoing, friendly personality exhibited, they make excellent pets and are excellent with children.

The Pharaoh is also a very intelligent and sensitive animal. He will sense his owners' moods, and the owner can often see the behavior of the dog affected by his own mood.

Pharaoh Hounds are also easier to train than most other hounds, and a person can train them for a variety of exercises and reasons. A friend has described how her uncle on Malta would hitch the dog to a cart, put a grocery list under the harness and send the dog off to the store. Later, the dog would return with the necessary parcels in the cart!

Description of the Breed

STANDARD FOR THE BREED

Each dog-registering organization draws up a standard for each of the breeds it recognizes. The wording in these standards may vary from country to country and from registry to registry. The following is the AKC standard for the Pharaoh Hound. Like all standards, it too can change from time to time. If you are serious about showing your dog, it would be wise to contact your local Pharaoh Hound club to acquire the most recent standard and any other relevant information.

The American Kennel Club and The Kennel Club of Great Britain have accepted standards for the Pharaoh Hound. It is not uncommon for these two standards to dissent on any number of points; however, in the case of the Pharaoh Hound, the standards agree nearly word for word. The American standard differs in its exclusion disregarding hunting wounds and in its height requirement for dogs, being one inch greater than the Kennel Club's 22-inch requirement.

General Appearance: is one of grace, power and speed. The Pharaoh Hound is medium sized, of noble bearing with hard clean-cut lines—graceful, well balanced, very fast with free easy movement and alert expression.

Head and Skull: Skull long, lean and chiseled. Foreface slightly longer than the skull. Only slight stop. Top of the skull parallel with the foreface

Even amidst the crowds and excitement of a dog show, the Pharaoh Hound can be remarkably well behaved.

representing a blunt wedge.

Nose—Flesh colored, blending with the coat. No other color.

Mouth—Powerful jaws with strong teeth. Scissor bite.

Eyes—Amber colored, blending with coat; oval, moderately deep set with keen intelligent expression.

Ears—Medium high set, carried erect when alert, but very mobile, broad at the base, fine and large.

Neck—Long, lean and muscular with a slight arch to carry the head on high. Clean throat line.

Body: Lithe with almost straight topline. Slight slope from croup to root of tail. Deep brisket almost down to point of elbow. Ribs well sprung. Moderate tuck up. Length of body from breast to haunch bone slightly longer than height of withers to ground.

Tail: Medium set, fairly thick at the base and tapering whip-like, reaching below the point of hock in repose. Well carried and curved when in action. The tail should not be tucked between the legs. A screw tail is a fault.

Despite his great speed and agility, the Pharaoh Hound can be quiet and unobtrusive in the home.

The Pharaoh Hound's appearance is one of power, grace, and speed.

Forequarters: Shoulders long and sloping and well laid back. Strong without being loaded. Forelegs straight and parallel. Elbows well tucked in. Pasterns strong.

Color: Ranging from tan/rich tan/chestnut with white markings allowed as follows: White tip on tail strongly desired. White on chest (called "the Star"). White on toes and slim white snip on center line of face permissible. Flecking or other white undesirable except for any solid white spot on the back of neck, shoulder, or any part of the back or sides of the dog, which is a disqualification.

Gait: Free and flowing; the head should be held fairly high and the dog should cover the ground well without any apparent effort. The legs and feet should move in line with the body; any tendency to throw the feet sideways or a high stepping "hackney" action is a definite fault.

Height: Dogs 23 inches to 25 inches. Bitches 21 inches to 24 inches. All over balance must be maintained.

Temperament: Intelligent, friendly, affectionate and playful.

Hindquarters: Strong and muscular. Moderate sweep of stifle. Well developed second thigh. Limbs parallel.

Feet: Neither cat nor hare but strong, well knuckled and firm, turning neither in nor out. Paws well padded. Dewclaws may be removed.

Coat: Short and glossy, ranging from fine and close to slightly harsh with no feathering. Accident blemishes should not be considered as faults. Alert and active. Very fast with a marked keenness for hunting, both by sight and scent.

The foregoing description is that of the ideal Pharaoh Hound. Any deviation from the above-described dog must be penalized to the extent of the deviation.

Disqualification: Any solid white spot on the back of neck, shoulder, or any part of the back or sides of the dog.

Effective January 1, 1984

Two Pharaoh Hounds engaged in a tug of war. Prospective Pharaoh owners should be aware that members of this breed need suitable outlets for their seemingly boundless energy.

Grooming the Pharaoh

With a shorthaired breed like the Pharaoh Hound, one might think that there would be no grooming involved; however, there are a few things that should be done to maintain a healthy dog, inside and out, in every breed.

An important part of grooming your Pharaoh is cutting nails. Try to clip them every week, especially during the show season. Lure coursing helps keep nails down somewhat, but they still need clipping on a regular basis.

Keep the Pharaoh's ears clean. With those upright, prick ears, Pharaoh Hounds do not have the ear problems that are common to drop-eared dogs. The ears should be cleaned

carefully and gently with a cotton swab at least once a week.

Speaking of cleaning, there are occasional odors which may occur in older dogs. The first item to check in older dogs would be the anal glands. You must also check the eyes, ears, and skin regularly.

With a shorthaired dog like a Pharaoh Hound, scrubbing and frequent bathing are not necessary or recommended. A sponge bath (with warm water) from time to time will help to keep your Pharaoh tidy. Follow with a brisk rub down with a heavy terry towel. If this is not effective, then resort to the complete bath. Be sure not to get water in their ears or

Pharaoh Hounds decked out in their best finery. These two models of canine high fashion are "Sunny" and "Tifla," owned by Sue M. Sefscik.

Grooming a Pharaoh is a relatively easy task, another of the assets of owning this breed. Owners, Mary M. McCormack and W. Valerie Rees.

soap in their eyes. Use a mild, natural soap and do not scrub roughly. Pharaohs have light skin, and it is not healthy to overscrub them. Of course, bathe only when absolutely necessary.

Do massage the Pharaoh with a nice hound glove; whether it is rubber or suede, it will remove loose hairs and also give the coat a nice shine. Brushing is too harsh for Pharaoh Hounds. A soft material such as a chamois also works well. Grooming should occur every week; after using the hound glove, coats are softer and silkier.

A good oil rinse or coat conditioner is also recommended. During the winter months (and especially with older pets), dry skin may develop. If such methods do not work, perhaps a diet supplement is necessary, especially if the condition persists. Naturally, no oils should be applied before a show.

It is not a good idea to use flea collars on Pharaohs since many of them have sensitive skin. The flea collars contain assorted chemicals which can affect the skin of a Pharaoh Hound and cause an allergic reaction.

The Pharaoh Hound's eagerness to please contributes to the breed's trainability, making it a good candidate for coursing, obedience, and hunting.

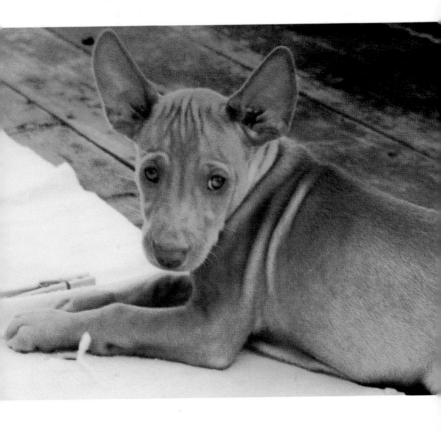

Groomers, veterinarians and pet stores have a variety of other products which will help control a flea problem.

Pharaohs can occasionally break a tail tip. If this should occur, a dry skin condition can lead to complications; therefore, when a tail has been injured, it should be kept lubricated until completely healed.

Pet quality or show quality, you will love your Pharaoh Hound for his even temperament and pleasant disposition.

Your veterinarian or pet shop dealer can recommend a product that will help to prevent the problem of dry skin.

A STEP-BY-STEP GROOMING PROCEDURE

The following procedure is designed to assist the Pharaoh Hound owner in grooming his dog. It has been approved by a panel of experts and is used by owners and groomers.

Tools and Equipment
- chamois
- hound glove
- ear cleaner
- medicated ear powder
- nail clipper (extra large)
- cotton balls
- coat conditioner
- tearless protein shampoo
- scissor
- skin cream

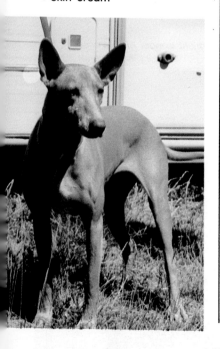

Procedure

1. Thoroughly massage the coat using a chamois or a hound glove.

2. Swab the ears with a cotton ball that has been moistened with ear cleaner. This will remove dirt and control ear odor. Follow with a dry cotton ball and dust the ears with medicated ear powder.

3. Cut the nails with a guillotine-type nail trimmer. Nails should be cut weekly.

4. Check between the foot pads and under the feet for burrs, tar, etc.

5. Bathe the dog with a tearless protein shampoo that is balanced pH-alkaline.

6. Cage dry until damp. Finish drying on the table, using a blow dryer and a chamois.

7. The whiskers may be removed with a scissor to improve expression, although this is optional.

8. Remove any long hair on the face.

9. To soften and heal calluses on the elbows, rub them with skin cream.

10. Finish with an oil rinse or coat conditioner to create a brilliant shine.

In the dog fancy, the Pharaoh Hound belongs to that group of dogs known as the Hound Group. Some other breeds in this group are the Afghan Hound, the Borzoi, and the Greyhound.

Versatility of the Breed

Unlike some other breeds of dog, the Pharaoh Hound is a very adaptable creature and is also very versatile. The Pharaoh can be shown in the American Kennel Club conformation ring in order to gain a title of "Champion." With relatively few Pharaohs in the United States, an owner-handler can do quite well in the show ring, even finishing a number of champions himself.

Naturally, along the lines of the AKC-recognized sports, one can also obedience train a Pharaoh. Although not as easy to train as some breeds, the Pharaoh is not too difficult despite his independent nature. The Pharaoh can be a happy working animal, provided the trainer-owner keeps a positive attitude as he trains. A number of beautiful Pharaohs have earned Companion Dog titles and have gone on to compete in Companion Dog Excellent rings. Perhaps in the near future, a Utility Dog title is in the wings!

Because the Pharaoh can work with both sight and scent, a Tracking Dog title is well within reach of most Pharaoh owners. Given the time and patience, one could easily put a Tracking Dog title on a Pharaoh.

Continuing with the versatility of the breed, there is an association unique to the

Even the most well-trained Pharaoh Hound might wander off if something captures his attention. Supervision of your pet when he is outdoors is but one aspect of responsible pet ownership.

sighthounds: American Field Sighthound Association (ASFA). The purpose of this organization is to continue the tradition of hunting sighthounds. Striving to keep the original purpose which hunters intended, ASFA trials are held in many places throughout the United States. Although not officially recognized by the AKC as yet, ASFA allows sighthound owners to work their dogs in the field, hunting by sight. It is done by allowing the hounds to chase

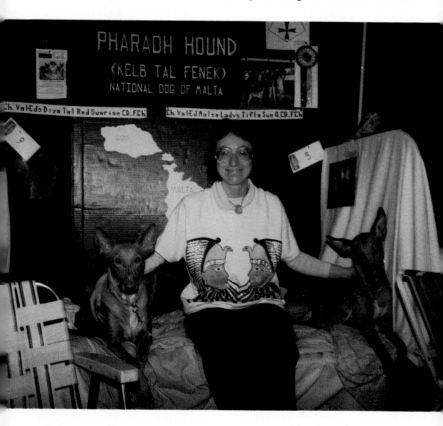

The author and her Ch. Val-Ed's Dija Tal Red Sunrise, C.D., and Ch. Val-Ed Malta Lady's Tifla Sue Q, C.D. Despite their independent natures, Pharaohs can be models of good behavior.

Facing page: *Some people think of Pharaohs as aloof, rather standoffish dogs. In actuality, they are friendly canines that can make fine pets. Owner, Rita L. Sacks.*

a plastic bag (lure) around a course that is intended to simulate live game running.

Pharaohs make excellent house pets and are extremely good with children. Many Pharaohs accompany their owners to pre-schools; they have also been used as therapy dogs in nursing homes. Some provide companionship for persons who would otherwise not be interested in life.

Being running dogs, Pharaoh Hounds need lots of physical exercise and stimulation.

Pharaohs can be seen jogging with their owners, chasing a ball along the beach or hunting on their own in the backyard (mainly grasshoppers and flies). Remembering their Maltese heritage, they make excellent rabbit hunters, provided they are trained and used properly, much the same as they are in their native Malta.

Some Pharaoh Hound owners prefer to keep their new pup in an enclosed area when it is time for their pet to rest or nap.

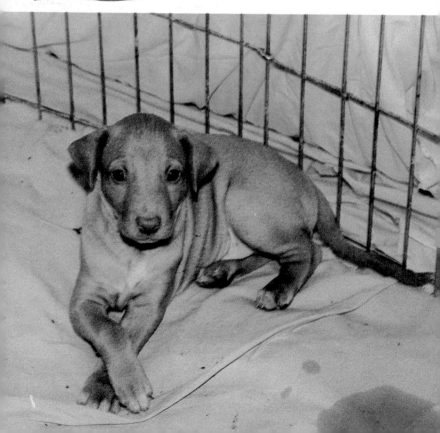

Selecting Your Dog

Now that you have decided which dog breed suits your needs, your lifestyle, and your own temperament, there will be much to consider before you make your final purchase. Buying a puppy on impulse may only cause heartbreak later on; it makes better sense to put some real thought into your canine investment, especially since it is likely that he will share many happy years with you. Which individual will you choose as your adoring companion? Ask yourself some questions as you analyze your needs and preferences for a dog, read all that you can about your particular breed, and visit as many dog shows as possible. At the shows you will be surrounded by people who can give you all the details about the breed you are interested in buying. Decide if you want a household pet, a dog for breeding, or a show dog. Would you prefer a male or female? Puppy or adult?

If you buy from a breeder, ask him to help you with your decision. When you have settled on the dog you want, discuss with him the dog's temperament, the animal's positive and negative aspects, any health problems it might have, its feeding and grooming requirements, and whether the dog has been immunized. Reputable breeders will be willing to answer any questions you might have that pertain to the dog you have selected, and often they will make themselves available if you call for advice or if you encounter problems after you've made your purchase.

Regular veterinary care, a proper diet, and exercise are important to your Pharaoh Hound's good health.

A bit too big?
A little **too** small.
Too fuzzy for me!
Too fat to crawl.

Before you wrap it tight
And crate it home,
Behold its appetite
And room to roam.

A sloppy yap, a barking slur,
Puppy eyes to be let free,
A him? a her? an unmarked cur,
Let's pout to see its pedigree.

The perfect pet quest:
Which pup for me is best?

ANDREW DE PRISCO

Most breeders want to see their dogs placed in loving, responsible homes; they are careful about who buys their animals. So as the dog's new owner, prepare yourself for some interrogation from the breeder.

WHERE TO BUY

You can choose among several places to buy your dog. Many people think of their local pet shop as the first source for buying a puppy, and very often they're

When selecting your Pharaoh Hound pup, look for one that is alert and interested in its surroundings. Also, be sure that you are given ample opportunity to hold your prospective new pet.

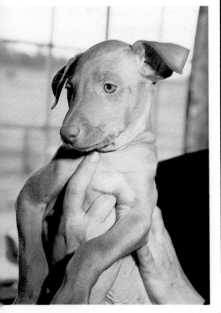

right; you should remember, however, that a pet shop cannot possibly stock all breeds of dog. If your pet shop does not carry the type of dog you desire, there are other places to look. One is a kennel whose business is breeding show-quality dogs; such kennels may have extra pups for sale. Another source is the one-dog owner who wants to sell the puppies from an occasional litter to pay the expenses of his small-scale breeding operation. To find such kennels and part-time breeders and hobbyists, check the classified section of your local newspaper or look in your telephone directory.

Whichever source you choose, you can usually tell in a very short time whether the puppies will make healthy and happy pets. If they are clean, plump, and lively, they are probably in good health. At the breeder's you will have the advantage of seeing the puppies' dam and perhaps their sire and other relatives. Remember that the mother, having just raised a demanding family, may not be looking her best; but if she is sturdy, friendly, and well-mannered, her puppies should be too. If you feel that something is lacking in the care or condition of the dogs, it is better to look elsewhere than to buy hastily and regret it afterward. Buy a healthy dog with a good disposition, one that has been

During their first few weeks of life, their mother's milk will provide all the nutrients these Pharaoh Hound puppies will need.

properly socialized and likes being around people.

If you cannot find the dog you want locally, write to the secretary of the national breed club or kennel club and ask for names of breeders near you or to whom you can write for information. Puppies are often shipped, sight unseen, from reputable breeders. In these instances, pictures and pedigree information are usually sent beforehand to help you decide.

Breeders can supply you with further details and helpful guidance, if you require it. Many breed clubs provide a puppy referral service, so you may want to look into this before making your final decision.

PET OR SHOW DOG

Conscientious breeders strive to maintain those desirable qualities in their breed. At the same time, they are always working to improve on what they have already achieved, and they do this by referring to the breed standard of perfection. The standard describes the ideal dog, and those animals that come close to the ideal are generally selected as show

Owners of purebred dogs too often forget that all breeds of dog are interrelated. The ancient canine that is the believed ancestor of all dogs is known as Tomarctus. As packs traveled and inhabited various lands, types evolved through the process of adaptation. Later, as dogs and man joined forces, type became further diversified. This chart sketches one commonly accepted theory of the domesticated dog's development. Where does your dog fit in? With a few exceptions, dogs evolve or change as a result of a specific functional need.

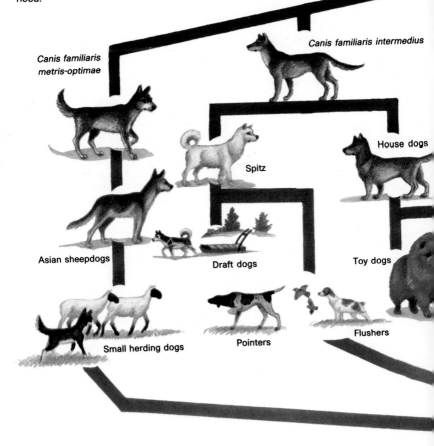

Canis familiaris intermedius

Canis familiaris metris-optimae

House dogs

Spitz

Asian sheepdogs

Draft dogs

Toy dogs

Small herding dogs

Pointers

Flushers

Tomarctus

Canis familiaris leineri

Canis familiaris inostranzewi

Russian Tracker

Molossian

Scenthounds

Sighthound
prototypes

Mastiffs

Sighthounds

Terriers

Bulldogs

Retrievers

Large herding dogs

stock; those that do not are culled and sold as pets. Keep in mind that pet-quality purebred dogs are in no way less healthy or attractive than show-quality specimens. It's just that the pet may have undesirable features (such as ears that are too large

For some Pharaoh Hound fanciers, nothing beats the excitement of having their dogs compete in coursing events.

or eyes that are the wrong color for its breed) which would be faults in the show ring. Often these so-called "flaws" are detectable only by experienced breeders or show judges. Naturally the more perfect animal, in terms of its breed standard, will cost more—even though he seems almost identical to his pet-quality littermate.

If you think you may eventually want to show your dog or raise a litter of puppies, by all means buy the best you can afford. You will save expense and disappointment later on. However, if the puppy is strictly to be a pet for the children, or a companion for you, you can afford to look for a bargain. The pup which is not show material, or the older pup for which there is often less demand, or the grown dog which is not being used for breeding are occasionally available and offer opportunities to save money. Remember that your initial investment may be a bargain, but it takes good food and care— and plenty of both—to raise a healthy, vigorous puppy through its adulthood.

Facing page: *Often mistaken for a Pharaoh is this dog: the Cirneco dell'Etna. In his native land of Italy, the Cirneco is used primarily for hunting.*

The price you pay for your dog is little compared to the love and devotion he will return over the many years he'll be with you. With proper care and affection, your pup should live to a ripe old age; thanks to modern veterinary science and improvements in canine nutrition, dogs today are better maintained and live longer. It is not uncommon to see dogs living well into their teens.

Generally speaking, small dogs live longer than big ones. With love and the proper care any dog will live to its optimum age. Many persons, however, opt for a particular breed because of its proven longevity. This, of course, is purely a personal decision.

MALE OR FEMALE

If you intend to breed your dog someday, by all means buy a female. You can find a suitable mate without difficulty when the time comes, and you'll have the pleasure of raising a litter of puppies. If you don't want to raise puppies, however, your female should be spayed so that she will remain a healthy, lively pet. Similarly, a male purchased as a pet, rather than as a stud

This illustration of the dog's skeleton and vital organs reveals the distinctive construction of the dog. Veterinary medicine, largely devoted to the better health of your dog, continues to make advances that promise even greater canine longevity.

According to some astrologers, dogs too are affected by their zodiac sign. If you follow the stars, be sure to select a dog born under a sky compatible with that of your birth date.

dog, should be castrated. The female is smaller than the male and generally quieter. She has less tendency to roam in search of romance, but a properly trained male can be a charming pet and has a certain difference in temperament that is appealing to many people. Male versus female is chiefly a matter of personal choice; both make fine companions.

ADULT OR PUP

Whether to buy a grown dog or a young puppy is another question. It is surely an undeniable pleasure to watch your dog grow from a lively pup to a mature, dignified dog. If you don't have the time to spend on the more frequent meals, housebreaking, and other training a puppy needs in order to become a dog you can be proud of, then choose an older, partly-trained adolescent or a grown dog. If you want a show dog, remember that no one, not even an expert, can predict with one hundred percent accuracy what a puppy will be like when he grows up. The dog may seem to exhibit show potential *most* of the time, but six months is the earliest age for the would-be exhibitor to select a prospect and know that its future is in the show ring.

If you have a small child, it is best to get a puppy big enough to defend itself, one not less than four or five months old.

Older children will enjoy playing with and helping to take care of a baby pup; but at less than four months, a puppy wants to do little else but eat and sleep, and he must be protected from teasing and overtiring. You cannot expect a very young child to understand that a puppy is a fragile living being; to the youngster he is a toy like his

Allowing your Pharaoh Hound up on the furniture is a matter of personal choice. Be sure to establish the "house rules" from the time you acquire your pet, and be consistent in enforcing them.

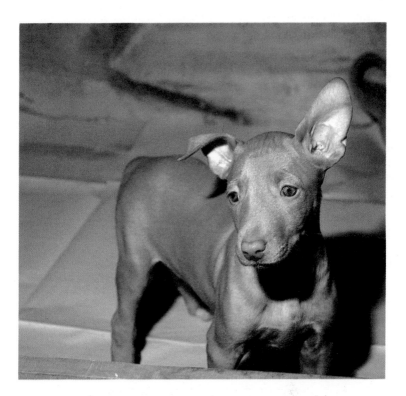

Give your new Pharaoh Hound pup ample opportunity to explore his new home.

stuffed dog. Children, therefore, must learn how to handle and care for their young pets.

We recommend you start with a puppy so that you can raise and train it according to the rules you have established in your own home. While a dog is young, its behavior can be more easily shaped by the owner, whereas an older dog , although trainable, may be a bit set in his ways.

WHAT TO LOOK FOR IN A PUPPY

In choosing a puppy, assuming that it comes from healthy, well-bred parents, look for one that is friendly and outgoing. The biggest pup in the litter is apt to be somewhat coarse as a grown dog, while the appealing "runt of the litter" may turn out to be a timid shadow—or have a Napoleonic complex! If you want a show dog and have no experience in choosing a prospect, study the breed standard and listen carefully to the breeder on the finer points of show conformation. A breeder's prices will be in accord with his puppies' expected worth, and he will be honest with you about each pup's potential because it is to his own advantage. He wants his top-quality show puppies placed in the public eye to reflect glory on him—and to attract future buyers. Why should he sell a potential show champion to someone who just wants a pet?

Now that you have paid your money and made your choice, you are ready to depart with puppy, papers, and instructions. Make sure that you know the youngster's feeding routine, and take along some of his food. For the trip home, place him in a comfortable, sturdy carrier. Do not drive home with a puppy on your lap! If you'll be travelling for a few hours, at the very least bring along a bottle of water from the breeder and a small water dish.

PEDIGREE AND REGISTRATION

Owners of puppies are often misled by sellers with such ruses as leading the owner to believe his dog is something special. The term *pedigree papers* is quite different from the term *registration papers*. A pedigree is nothing more than a statement made by the breeder of the dog;

Dog shows are fascinating to both the participants and the spectators. If you have never attended a dog show, you are missing an important part of the canine world. This is the Crufts Show in England.

Pedigree papers can trace a dog's lineage back several generations. They do not, however, guarantee that a puppy is of good quality or sound health.

and it is written on special pedigree blanks, which are readily available from any pet shop or breed club, with the names of several generations from which the new puppy comes. It records your puppy's ancestry and other important data, such as the pup's date of birth, its breed, its sex, its sire and dam, its breeder's name and address, and so on. If your dog has had purebred champions in his background, then the pedigree papers are valuable as evidence of the good breeding behind your dog; but if the names on the pedigree paper are

meaningless, then so is the paper itself. Just because a dog has a pedigree doesn't necessarily mean he is registered with a kennel club.

Registration papers from the American Kennel Club or the United Kennel Club in the United States or The Kennel Club of Great Britain attest to the fact that the mother and father of your puppy were purebred dogs of the breed represented by your puppy and that they were registered with a particular club. Normally every registered dog also has a complete pedigree available. Registration papers, which you receive when you buy a puppy, merely enable you to register your puppy. Usually the breeder has registered only the litter, so it is the new owner's responsibility to register and name an individual pup. The papers should be filled out and sent to the appropriate address printed on the application, along with the fee required for the registration. A certificate of registration will then be sent to you.

Pedigree and registration, by the way, have nothing to do with licensing, which is a local regulation applying to purebred and mongrel alike. Find out what the local ordinance is in your town or city and how it applies to your dog; then buy a license and keep it on your dog's collar for identification.

As stunning as any rose from Cairo are "Tifla" and "Sunny," pictured with the author.

The New Family Member

A Pharaoh Hound in motion is truly a beautiful sight to behold. Shown are Ch. Lileo's Melita of Phaererin and Ch. Val-Ed's Dija Tal Red Sunrise, C.D.

At long last, the day you have all been waiting for, your new puppy will make its grand entrance into your home. Before you bring your companion to its new residence, however, you must plan carefully for its arrival. Keep in mind that the puppy will need

The New Family Member

time to adjust to life with a different owner. He may seem a bit apprehensive about the strange surroundings in which he finds himself, having spent the first few weeks of life with his dam and littermates, but in a couple of days, with love and patience on your part, the transition will be complete.

First impressions are important, especially from the puppy's point of view, and these may very well set the pattern of his future relationship with you. You must be consistent in the

A crate, for home and travel, is standard equipment and makes an excellent gift for the new dog owner.

way you handle your pet so that he learns what is expected of him. He must come to trust and respect you as his keeper and master. Provide him with proper care and attention, and you will be rewarded with a loyal companion for many years. Considering the needs of your puppy and planning ahead will surely make the change from his former home to his new one easier.

ADVANCE PREPARATION

In preparing for your puppy's arrival, perhaps more important than anything else is to find out from the seller how the pup was maintained. What brand of food was offered and when and how often was the puppy fed? Has the pup been housebroken; if so, what method was employed? Attempt to continue whatever routine was started by the person from whom you bought your puppy; then, gradually, you can make those changes that suit you and your lifestyle. If, for example, the puppy has been paper trained, plan to stock up on newspaper. Place this newspaper toilet facility in a selected spot so that your puppy learns to use the designated area as his "bathroom." And keep on hand a supply of the dog food to which he is accustomed, as a sudden switch to new food could cause digestive upsets.

Another consideration is sleeping and resting quarters. Be sure to supply a dog bed for your pup, and introduce him to his special cozy corner so that he

A warm bed, equipped with a ticking clock, chew bone, and safe dog toy, can help a pup feel secure and welcome in its new home.

knows where to retire when he feels like taking a snooze. You'll need to buy a collar (or harness) and leash, a safe chew item (such as Nylabone® or Gumabone®), and a few grooming tools as well. A couple of sturdy feeding dishes, one for food and one for water, will be needed; and it will be necessary, beforehand, to set up a feeding station.

FINDING A VETERINARIAN

An important part of your preparations should include finding a local veterinarian who can provide quality health care in the form of routine check-ups, inoculations, and prompt medical attention in case of illness or an emergency. Find out if the animal you have selected has been vaccinated against canine diseases, and make certain you secure all health certificates at the time of purchase. This information will be valuable to your veterinarian, who will want to know the puppy's complete medical history. Incidentally, don't wait until your puppy becomes sick before you seek the services of a vet; make an appointment for your pup before or soon after he takes up residence with you so that he starts out with a clean bill of health in his new home.

CHILDREN AND PUPPIES

Prepare the young members of the household on pet care. Children should learn not only to love their charges but to respect them and treat them with the consideration one would give all living things. It must be emphasized to youngsters that the puppy has certain needs, just as humans have, and all family members must take an active role in ensuring that these needs are met. Someone must feed the puppy. Someone must walk him a couple of times a day or clean up after him if he is trained to relieve himself on newspaper. Someone must groom his coat, clean his ears, and clip his nails from time to time. Someone

must see to it that the puppy gets sufficient exercise and attention each day.

A child who has a pet to care for learns responsibility; nonetheless, parental guidance is an essential part of his learning experience. Many a child has been known to "love a pet to death," squeezing and hugging the animal in ways which are irritating or even painful. Others have been found guilty of teasing, perhaps unintentionally, and disturbing their pet while the animal is eating or resting. One must teach a child, therefore, when and how to gently stroke and fondle a puppy. In time, the child can learn how to carefully pick up and handle the pup. A dog should always be supported with both hands, *not* lifted by the scruff of the neck. One hand placed under the chest, between the front legs, and the other hand supporting the dog's rear end will be comfortable and will restrain the animal as you hold and carry him. Always demonstrate to children the proper way to lift a dog.

BE A GOOD NEIGHBOR

For the sake of your dog's safety and well being, don't allow him to wander onto the property of others. Keep him confined at all times to your own yard or indoors where he won't become a nuisance. Consider what

Note the keenly alert expressions on the faces of this pair of Pharaoh Hounds. Owners, Nick and Michele Calamaras.

Many dangers lurk around the house. Keep all poisonous substances and sharp objects away from your curious pup.

dangers lie ahead for an unleashed dog that has total freedom of the great outdoors, particularly when he is unsupervised by his master. There are cars and trucks to dodge on the streets and highways. There are stray animals with which to wrangle. There are poisons all around, such as car antifreeze in driveways or toxic plants and shrubs, which, if swallowed, could prove fatal. There are dognappers and sadistic people who may steal or bring harm to your beloved pet. In short, there are all sorts of nasty things

waiting to hurt him. Did you know that if your dog consumes rotting garbage, there is the possibility he could go into shock or even die? And are you aware that a dog left to roam in a wooded area or field could become infected with any number of parasites if he plays with or ingests some small prey, such as a rabbit, that might be carrying these parasitic organisms? A thorn from a rosebush imbedded in the dog's foot pad, tar from a newly paved road stuck to his coat, and a wound inflicted by a wild animal all can be avoided if you take the precaution of keeping your dog in a safe enclosure where he will be protected from such dangers. Don't let your dog run loose; he is likely to stray from home and get into all sorts of trouble.

Clockwise from upper right: *pokeweed, jimson weed, foxglove,* and *yew. If ingested, a toxic plant can be dangerous to your dog.*

The New Family Member

GETTING ACQUAINTED

Plan to bring your new pet home in the morning so that by nightfall he will have had some time to become acquainted with you and his new environment. Avoid introducing the pup to the family around holiday time, since all of the extra excitement will only add to the confusion and frighten him. Let the puppy enter your home on a day when the

Resist the temptation to handle him too much during these first few days. And, if there are other dogs or animals around the house, make certain all are properly introduced. If you observe fighting among the animals, or some other problem, you may have to separate all parties until they learn to accept one another. Remember that neglecting your other pets while

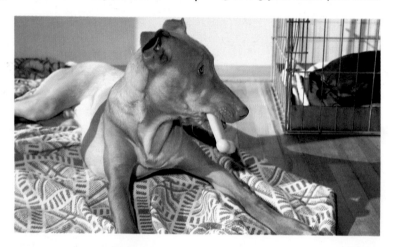

routine is normal. For those people who work during the week, a Saturday morning is an ideal time to bring the puppy to his new home; this way he has the entire weekend to make adjustments before being left alone for a few hours, come Monday morning.

Let the puppy explore, under your watchful eye of course, and let him come to know his new home without stress and fear.

An important part of caring for your Pharaoh Hound involves supplying him with a safe, durable chewing aid such as a Nylabone®.

Facing page: *The coat of the Pharaoh is short and glossy. Co-owners, Mary M. McCormack and Valerie Rees.*

showering the new puppy with extra attention will only cause animosity and jealousy. Make an effort to pay special attention to the other animals as well.

On that eventful first night, try not to give in and let the puppy sleep with you; otherwise, this could become a difficult habit to break. Let him cry and whimper, even if it means a night of restlessness for the entire family. Some people have had success with putting a doll or a hot water bottle wrapped in a towel in the puppy's bed as a surrogate mother, while others have placed a ticking alarm clock in the bed to simulate the heartbeat of the pup's dam and littermates. Remember that this furry little fellow is used to the warmth and security of his mother and siblings, so the adjustment to sleeping alone will take time. Select a location away from drafts and away from the feeding station for placement of his dog bed. Keep in mind, also, that the bed should be roomy enough for him to stretch out in; as he grows older, you may need to supply a larger one.

Prior to the pup's arrival, set up his room and partition it the way you would to keep an infant out of a particular area. You may want to keep his bed, his feeding station, and his toilet area all in the same room—in separate locations—or you may want to set the feeding station up in your kitchen, where meals for all family members are served. Whatever you decide, do it ahead of time so you will have that much less to worry about when your puppy finally moves in with you.

Above all else, be patient with your puppy as he adjusts to life in his new home. If you purchase a pup that is not housebroken, you will have to spend time with the dog—just as you would with a small child—until he develops proper toilet habits. Even a housebroken puppy may feel nervous in strange new surroundings and have an occasional accident. Praise and encouragement will elicit far better results than punishment or scolding. Remember that your puppy wants nothing more than to please you, thus he is anxious to learn the behavior that is required of him.

Feeding Requirements

Perhaps more than any other single aspect of your dog's development, proper feeding requires an educated and responsible dog owner. The importance of nutrition on your dog's bone and muscle growth cannot be over emphasized.

Soon after your puppy comes to live with you, he will need to be fed. Remember to ask the seller what foods were given to the youngster and stay with that diet for a while. It is important for the puppy to keep eating and to avoid skipping a meal, so entice him with the food to which he is accustomed. If you prefer to switch to some other brand of dog food, each day begin to add small quantities of the new brand to the usual food offering. Make the portions of the new food progressively larger until the pup is weaned from his former diet.

What should you feed the puppy and how often? His diet is really quite simple and relatively inexpensive to prepare. Puppies need to be fed small portions at frequent intervals, since they are growing and their activity level is high. You must ensure that your pup gains weight steadily; with an adult dog, however, growth slows down and weight must be regulated to prevent obesity and a host of other problems. At one time, it was thought that home-cooked meals were the answer, with daily rations of meat,

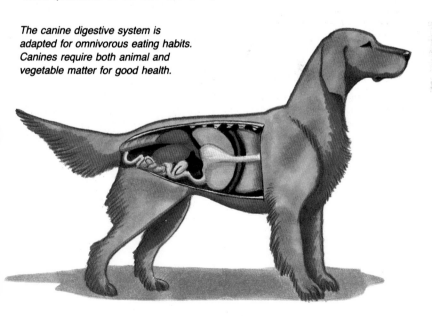

The canine digestive system is adapted for omnivorous eating habits. Canines require both animal and vegetable matter for good health.

vegetables, egg yolk, cereal, cheese, brewer's yeast, and vitamin supplements. With all of the nutritionally complete commercial dog food products readily available, these time-consuming preparations really are unnecessary now. A great deal of money and research has resulted in foods that we can serve our dogs with confidence and pride; and most of these commercial foods have been developed along strict guidelines according to the size, weight, and age of your dog. These products are reasonably priced, easy to find, and convenient to store.

THE PUPPY'S MEALS

After a puppy has been fully weaned from its mother until approximately three months of age, it needs to be fed four times a day. In the morning and evening offer kibble (dog meal) soaked in hot water or broth, to which you have added some canned meat-based food or fresh raw meat cut into small chunks. At noon and bedtime feed him a bit of kibble or whole-grain cereal moistened with milk (moistening, by the way, makes the food easier to digest, since dogs don't typically chew their food). From three to six months, increase the portion size and

Pharaoh Hound pups can be fed small amounts of food several times a day. As they mature, portions should be larger but the number of meals per day less.

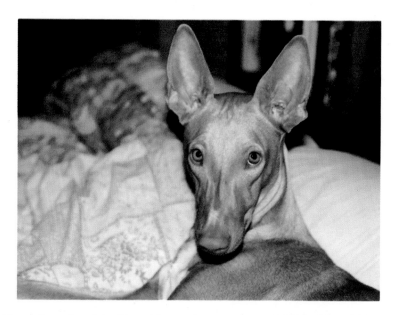

The amber color of the Pharaoh's eyes blends with his coat.

offer just three meals—one milk and two meat. At six months, two meals are sufficient; at one year, a single meal can be given, supplemented with a few dry biscuits in the morning and evening. During the colder months, especially if your dog is active, you might want to mix in some wheat germ oil or corn oil or bacon drippings with the meal to add extra calories. Remember to keep a bowl of cool, fresh water on hand always to help your dog regulate its body temperature and to aid in digestion.

From one year on, you may continue feeding the mature dog a single meal (in the evening, perhaps, when you have your supper), or you may prefer to divide this meal in two, offering half in the morning and the other half at night. Keep in mind that while puppies require foods in small chunks, or nuggets, older dogs can handle larger pieces of food at mealtime. Discuss your dog's feeding schedule with your veterinarian; he can make suggestions about the right diet for your particular canine friend.

COMPARISON SHOPPING
With so many fine dog-food products on the market today, there is something for

Feeding Requirements

everyone's pet. You may want to serve dry food "as is" or mix it with warm water or broth. Perhaps you'll choose to combine dry food with fresh or canned preparations. Some canned foods contain all meat, but they are not complete; others are mixtures of meat and grains, which have been fortified with additional nutrients to make them more complete and balanced. There are also various packaged foods that can be served alone or as supplements and that can be left out for a few hours without spoiling. This self-feeding method, which works well for dogs that are not prone to weight problems, allows the animal to serve himself whenever he feels hungry. Many people who work during the day find these dry or semi-moist rations convenient to use, and these foods are great to bring along if you travel with your dog.

Be sure to read the labels carefully before you make your dog-food purchases. Most

Pet shops offer a large selection of quality bowls that are efficient and affordable. Offered in a wide variety of colors, bowls are easy to coordinate.

Vegetables, grains, meats and dairy products are all vital components of your dog's diet. Fortunately, commercial dog foods are nutritionally balanced and easily digestible.

reputable pet-food manufacturers list the ingredients and the nutritional content right on the can or package. Instructions are usually included so that you will know how much to feed your dog to keep him thriving and in top condition. A varied, well-balanced diet that supplies the proper amounts of protein, carbohydrate, fat, vitamins, minerals, and water is important to keep your puppy healthy and to guarantee his normal development. Adjustments to the diet can be made, under your veterinarian's supervision, according to the individual puppy, his rate of growth, his activity level, and so on. Liquid or powder vitamin and mineral supplements, or those in tablet form, are available and can be given if you need to feel certain that the diet is balanced.

Intelligent, friendly, and alert, a Pharaoh Hound is a good choice as a canine companion.

DEVELOPING GOOD EATING HABITS

Try to serve your puppy his meals at the same time each day and in the same location so that he will get used to his daily routine and develop good eating habits. A bit of raw egg, cottage cheese, or table scraps (leftover food from your own meals) can

Feeding your dog need not be a messy chore, provided that non-tipping, easy-clean bowls are used for each meal.

be offered from time to time; but never accustom your dog to eating human "junk food." Cake, candy, chocolate, soda, and other snack foods are for people, not dogs. Besides, these foods provide only "empty" calories that your pet doesn't need if he is to stay healthy. Avoid offering spicy, fried, fatty, or starchy foods; rather, offer leftover meats, vegetables, and gravies. Get in the habit of feeding your puppy or your grown dog his *own* daily meals of dog food. If ever you are in doubt about what foods and how much to serve, consult your veterinarian.

Feeding Requirements

A pet nurser enables you to feed pups that have difficulty nursing from their mother and also helps with the weaning process.

FEEDING GUIDELINES

Some things to bear in mind with regard to your dog's feeding regimen follow.

- Nutritional balance, provided by many commercial dog foods, is vital; avoid feeding a one-sided all-meat diet. Variety in the kinds of meat (beef, lamb, chicken, liver) or cereal grains (wheat, oats, corn) that you offer your dog is of secondary importance compared to the balance or "completeness" of dietary components.

- Always refrigerate opened canned food so that it doesn't spoil. Remember to remove all uneaten portions of canned or moistened food from the feeding dish as soon as the pup has finished his meal. Discard the leftover food immediately and thoroughly wash and dry the feeding dish, as a dirty dish is a breeding ground for harmful germs.

- When offering dry foods, always keep a supply of water on hand for your dog. Water should be made available at all times, even if dry foods are not left out for self-feeding. Each day the water dish should be washed with soap and hot water, rinsed well, and dried; a refill of clean, fresh water should be provided daily.

- Food and water should be served at room temperature, neither too hot nor too cold, so that it is more palatable for your puppy.

- Serve your pup's meals in sturdy hard-plastic, stainless steel, or earthenware containers, ones that won't tip over as the dog gulps his food down. Some bowls and dishes are weighted to prevent spillage, while others fit neatly into holders which offer support. Feeding dishes should be large enough to hold each meal.

- Whenever the nutritional needs of your dog change—

that is to say, when it grows older or if it becomes ill, obese, or pregnant; or if it starts to nurse its young—special diets are in order. Always contact your vet for advice on these special dietary requirements.

- Feed your puppy at the same regular intervals each day; reserve treats for special

given the chance, he will accept and relish every in-between-meal tidbit you offer him. This pampering will only put extra weight on your pet and cause him to be unhealthy in the long run.

- Do not encourage your dog to beg for food from the table while you are eating your meals.

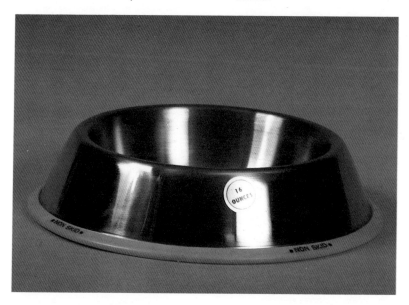

occasions or, perhaps, to reward good behavior during training sessions.

- Hard foods, such as biscuits and dog meal, should be offered regularly. Chewing on these hard, dry morsels helps the dog keep its teeth clean and its gums conditioned.
- Never overfeed your dog. If

Metal bowls are long lasting and easy to clean. Feeding and water bowls should be washed with soap and warm water and then rinsed on a regular basis.

FEEDING CHART

Age and No. of Feedings Per Day	Weight in Lbs.	Weight in Kg.	Caloric Requirement kcal M.E./Day
Puppies—Weaning to 3 months Four per day	1–3	.5–1.4	124–334
	3–6	1.4–2.7	334–574
	6–12	2.7–5.4	574–943
	12–20	5.4–9.1	943–1384
	15–30	6.8–13.6	1113–1872
Puppies—3 to 6 months Three per day	3–10	1.4–4.5	334–816
	5–15	2.3–6.8	494–1113
	12–25	5.4–11.3	943–1645
	20–40	9.1–18.2	1384–2352
	30–70	13.6–31.8	1872–3542
Puppies—6 to 12 months Two per day	6–12	2.7–5.4	574–943
	12–25	5.4–11.3	943–1645
	20–50	9.1–22.7	1384–2750
	40–70	18.2–31.8	2352–3542
	70–100	31.8–45.4	3542–4640
Normally Active Adults One or two per day	6–12	2.7–5.4	286–472
	12–25	5.4–11.3	472–823
	25–50	11.3–22.7	823–1375
	50–90	22.7–40.8	1375–2151
	90–175	40.8–79.4	2151–3675

This chart presents general parameters of a dog's caloric requirements, based on weight. The total caloric intake comes from a complete, balanced diet of quality foods. To assist owners, dog food companies generally provide the nutritional information of their product right on the label.

Accommodations

Puppies newly weaned from their mother and siblings should be kept warm at all times. As they get older, they can be acclimated gradually to cooler temperatures. When you purchase your dog, find out from the seller whether he is hardy and can withstand the rigors of outdoor living. Many breeds have been known to adapt well to a surprising number of invest in a crate for him to call his "home" whenever he needs to be confined for short intervals. You might plan to partition off a special room, or part of a room, for your pooch; or you may find that a heated garage or finished basement works well as your dog's living quarters. If your breed can tolerate living outside, you may want to buy or build him his own dog house with an

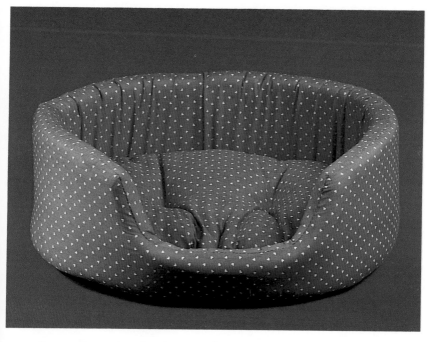

environments, so long as they are given time to adjust. If your pup is to be an indoor companion, perhaps a dog bed in the corner of the family room will suffice; or you may want to

A bed for your dog gives him a place to call his own. His bed should be placed in a warm, dry, draft-free location.

Accommodations

attached run. It might be feasible to place his house in your fenced-in backyard. The breed that can live outdoors fares well when given access to some sort of warm, dry shelter during periods of inclement weather. As you begin thinking about where your canine friend will spend most of his time, you'll want to consider his breed, his age, his temperament, his need for exercise, and the money, space, and resources you have available to house him.

THE DOG BED

In preparing for your puppy's arrival, it is recommended that a dog bed be waiting for him so that he has a place to sleep and rest. If you have provided him with his own bed or basket, ensure that it is placed in a warm, dry, draft-free spot that is private but at the same time near the center of family activity. Refrain from placing his bed near the feed and water dishes or his toilet area. You may want to give your puppy something with

Dog beds come in a variety of sizes and styles and are easily acquired at your local pet shop. Choose one that will accommodate your puppy when he has reached his full-grown size.

which to snuggle, such as a laundered towel or blanket or an article of old clothing. Some dogs have been known to chew apart their beds and bedding, but you can easily channel this chewing energy into more constructive behavior simply by supplying him with some safe toys or a Nylabone® pacifier for gnawing. Pet shops stock dog beds, among other supplies that you might need for your pup. Select a bed that is roomy, comfortable, and easy to clean, keeping in mind that you may have to replace the smaller bed with a larger one as the puppy grows to adulthood. Remember to clean and disinfect the bed and sleeping area from time to time, as these can become parasitic playgrounds for fleas, lice, mites, and the like.

Accommodations

THE CRATE

Although many dog lovers may cringe at the mere mention of the word *crate,* thinking of it as a cage or a cruel means of confinement, this handy piece of equipment can be put to good use for puppies and grown dogs alike. Even though you may love your dog to an extraordinary degree, you may not want him to have free rein of the house, particularly when you are not home to supervise him. If used properly, a crate can restrict your dog when it is not convenient to have him underfoot, *i.e.,* when guests are visiting or during your mealtimes.

A surprising number of dog owners, who originally had negative feelings about crating their dogs, have had great success using crates. The crate itself serves as a bed, provided it is furnished with bedding material, or it can be used as an indoor dog house. Not all dogs readily accept crates or being confined in them for short intervals, so for these dogs, another means of restriction must be found. But for those dogs that do adjust to spending

Crates allow for safe and easy travel and aid in the housebreaking process. Crates come in a variety of sizes, styles and colors.

time in these structures, the crate can be useful in many ways. The animal can be confined for a few hours while you are away from home or at work, or you can bring your crated dog along with you in the car when you travel or go on vacation. Crates also prove handy as carriers whenever you have to transport a sick dog to the veterinarian.

Most crates are made of sturdy wire or plastic, and some of the collapsible models can be conveniently stored or folded so that they can be moved easily from room to room or from inside the house to the yard on a warm, sunny day. If you allow your puppy or grown dog to become acquainted with its crate by cleverly propping the door open and leaving some of his favorite toys inside, in no time he will come to regard the crate as his own doggie haven. As with a dog bed, place the crate away from drafts in a dry, warm spot; refrain from placing food and water dishes in it, as these only crowd the space and offer opportunity for spillage.

If you need to confine your puppy so that he can't get into mischief while you're not home, remember to consider the animal's needs at all times. Select a large crate, one in which the dog can stand up and move around comfortably; in fact, bigger is better in this context.

The crate you choose for your dog should be appropriately sized. A crate can provide the new pet with a sense of security and belonging. Easily accessible, crates are an inexpensive, sensible investment.

Never leave the animal confined for more than a few hours at a time without letting him out to exercise, play, and, if necessary, relieve himself. Never crate a dog for ten hours, for example, unless you keep the door to the crate open so that he can get out for food and water and to stretch a bit. If long intervals of confinement are necessary, consider placing the unlatched crate in a partitioned section of your house or apartment.

Crates have become the answer for many a dog owner faced with the dilemma of either

Accommodations

getting rid of a destructive dog or living with him despite his bad habits. People who have neither the time nor the patience to train their dogs, or to modify undesirable behavior patterns, can at least restrain their pets during the times they can't be there to supervise. So long as the crate is used in a humane fashion, whereby a dog is confined for no more than a few hours at any one time, it can figure importantly in a dog owner's life. Show dogs, incidentally, learn at an early age that much time will be spent in and out of crates while they are on the show circuit. Many canine celebrities are kept in their crates until they are called to ringside, and they spend many hours crated to and from the shows.

THE DOG HOUSE

These structures, often made of wood, should be sturdy and

Consider your dog's present and fully grown size before purchasing the proper crate for him.

Commercial dog houses are designed for comfort and pest control.

offer enough room for your dog to stretch out in when it rests or sleeps. Dog houses that are elevated or situated on a platform protect the animal from cold and dampness that may seep through the ground. Of the breeds that are temperature hardy and will live outdoors, some are housed outside during the daytime only; others are permanent outdoor residents day and night, all year 'round.

If your intention is to have a companion that lives out-of-doors, it will be necessary to provide him with a more elaborate house, one that really protects him from the elements. Make sure the dog's house is constructed of waterproof materials. Furnish him with sufficient bedding to burrow into on a chilly night and provide extra insulation to keep out drafts and wet weather. Add a partition (a kind of room divider which separates the entry area from the main sleeping space) inside his house or attach a swinging door to the entrance to help keep him warm when he is

Accommodations

inside his residence. The swinging door facilitates entry to and from the dog house, while at the same time it provides protection, particularly from wind and drafts.

Some fortunate owners whose yards are enclosed by high fencing allow their dogs complete freedom within the boundaries of their property. In these situations, a dog can leave his dog house and get all the exercise he wants. Of course such a large space requires more effort to keep it clean. An alternative to complete backyard freedom is a dog kennel or run which attaches to or surrounds the dog's house. This restricts some forms of movement, such as running, perhaps, but it does provide ample room for walking, climbing, jumping, and stretching. Another option is to fence off part of the yard and place the dog house in the enclosure. If you need to tether your dog to its house, make certain to use a fairly long lead so as not to hamper the animal's need to move and exercise his limbs.

A thick drape hung over the entrance to the dog's house will prevent drafts, thus keeping your dog warm and dry.

CLEANLINESS

No matter where your dog lives, either in or out of your home, be sure to keep him in surroundings that are as clean and sanitary as possible. His excrement should be removed and disposed of every day without fail. No dog should be forced to lie in his own feces. If your dog lives in his own house, the floor should be swept occasionally and the bedding should be changed regularly if it becomes soiled. Food and water dishes need to be scrubbed with hot water and detergent and rinsed well to remove all traces of soap. The water dish should be refilled with a supply of fresh water. The dog and his environment must be kept free of parasites (especially fleas and mosquitoes, which can carry disease) with products designed to keep these pests under control. Dog crates need frequent scrubbing, too, as do the floors of kennels and runs. Your pet must be kept clean and comfortable at all times; if you exercise strict sanitary control, you will keep disease and parasite infestation to a minimum.

Just as grooming and bathing keep your dog in a healthy condition, regular cleaning and disinfecting of his living area are important for his overall health. Many dogs that suffer from depression are subjected to

More and more cities and towns are requiring dog owners to clean up after their pets. Commercial pooper scoopers can make the clean-up easy and efficient. They are also helpful for backyard sanitation.

poorly maintained quarters. Your dog's physical and psychological well being are closely related. A clean dog is a healthy and happy dog.

Accommodations

EXERCISE

A well-balanced diet and regular medical attention from a qualified veterinarian are essential in promoting good health for your dog, but so is daily exercise to keep him fit and mentally alert. Dogs that have been confined all day while their owners are at work or school need special attention. There should be some time set aside make this daily ritual more pleasant both for themselves and their canine companions by combining the walk with a little "roughhousing," that is to say, a bit of fun and togetherness.

Whenever possible, take a stroll to an empty lot, a playground, or a nearby park. Attach a long lead to your dog's collar, and let him run and jump and tone his body through

Large outdoor pens are used by many breeding, boarding, and medical professionals. Always inspect the facility before leaving your dog in any professional's care.

each day for play—a romp with a family member, perhaps. Not everyone is lucky enough to let his dog run through an open meadow or along a sandy beach, but even a ten-minute walk in the fresh air will do. Dogs that are house-bound, particularly those that live in apartments, need to be walked out-of-doors after each meal so that they can relieve themselves. Owners can aerobic activity. This will help him burn calories and will keep him trim, and it will also help relieve tension and stress that may have had a chance to develop while you were away all day. For people who work Monday through Friday, weekend jaunts can be especially beneficial, since there will be more time to spend with your canine friend. You might

Responsible breeding practices, regular exercise, and proper nutrition all contribute to sound bone development.

want to engage him in a simple game of fetch with a stick or a rubber ball. Even such basic tricks as rolling over, standing on the hindlegs, or jumping up (all of which can be done inside the home as well) can provide additional exercise. But if you plan to challenge your dog with a real workout to raise his heart rate, remember not to push him too hard without first warming up with a brisk walk. Don't forget to "cool him down" afterwards with a rhythmic trot until his heart rate returns to normal. Some dog owners jog with their dogs or take them along on bicycle excursions.

At the very least, however, play with your dog every day to keep him in good shape physically and mentally. If you can walk him outdoors, or better yet run with him in a more vigorous activity, by all means do it. Don't neglect your pet and leave him confined

The knee joint is also known as the stifle joint. It is formed by the articulation of the upper and lower leg.

for long periods without attention from you or time for exercise.

EXERCISING FOR YOU AND YOUR DOG

Dogs are like people. They come in three weights: overweight, underweight, and the correct weight. It is fair to say that most dogs are in better shape than most humans who own them. The reason for this is that most dogs accept exercise without objection—people do not! Follow your dog's lead towards exercise and the complete enjoyment of the outdoors—your dog is the ideal work-out partner. There are toys at your local pet shop which are designed just for that purpose: to allow you to play and exercise with your dog. Here are a few recommended exercise toys for you and your dog.

Flying discs can make exercise exciting.

Frisbee® Flying Discs*

Who hasn't seen or heard of a Frisbee® flying disc? This flying-saucer–like toy is available in three or more sizes. The small size is 10 cm (4″); the medium size is about 15 cm (6″) and the larger size is 23 cm (9″). The size of the flying disc has little to do with the size of the dog—small puppies chase anything; some larger dogs chase nothing. The advantage of the larger disc is that it is the same size as the toy made for humans only! Start with the size that you think is best suited for your dog. What is much more important is the material from which the flying disc is made; *soft un-chew-worthy plastic flying discs are not good for dogs.*

Most people play with these polyethylene discs and use these same discs to play with their dogs. Polyethylene plastic discs usually last an hour or so. Every time the dog grabs it, his teeth dig into the cheap plastic, leaving an imprint. In a short while the disc is not useable— and even worse, it may be dangerous, since the dog can break off a chunk and swallow it, or the distorted disc can swerve out of control and hit someone.

*Frisbee® is a trademark of the Kransco Company, California, and is used for their brand of flying disc.

Be sure that you do not throw the flying disc where your dog can injure himself. Open spaces where cars are not permitted or a park are most ideal.

Nylon Discs

Your pet shop will have a nylon disc that has a dog bone molded into the top of it. While this may look silly at first, the advantage is simple. When a typical Frisbee® lands on a flat surface, the dog may be unable to grasp it with its mouth or turn it over with its paw. Thus frustrated, the dog loses interest in the game and you will have to fetch it yourself. The nylon disc with the bone molded into the top of it allows the dog the option of flipping it over with its paw or grasping it with its mouth. It also has more capacity; thus you can use it as a food or water dish on these outings. The nylon disc may also be flavored and scented, besides being annealed, so your dog can find it more easily if it gets lost in the woods or high grass.

Polyurethane Flexible Floppy Flying Discs

The greatest advance in flying discs came with the manufacture of these discs from polyurethane. The polyurethane is so soft that it doesn't hurt you, your dog, or the window it might strike accidentally. Only very, very rarely can it break a window—usually one that was already cracked. The polyurethane Gumadisc® is floppy and soft. It can be folded

Gumabone® flying discs are proven safe and durable for dogs. The soft, pliable texture and the scent impregnation make these discs loved by dogs.

and fits into your pocket. It is also much tougher than cheap plastics, and most pet shops guarantee that it will last ten times longer than cheap plastic discs.

With most flying discs made for dogs comes an instruction booklet on how to use the disc with your canine friend. Basically, you play with the dog and the disc so the dog knows the disc belongs to him. Then you throw it continuously, increasing the distance, so that the dog fetches it and brings it back to you.

The exercise for you comes in when your dog stops fetching it, or when you have a partner. The two of you play catch. You stand as far apart as available space allows—usually 30–35 m (100 feet) is more than enough room. You throw the disc to each other, arousing your dog's interest as he tries to catch it. When the disc is dropped or veers off, the dog grabs it and brings it back (hopefully). Obviously you will have to run to catch the disc before your dog does.

There are contests held all over the world where distance, height, and other characteristics are measured competitively. Ask your local pet shop to help you locate a Frisbee® Club near you.

*Frisbee® is a trademark of the Kransco Company, California, and is used for their brand of flying disc.

Many owners complain that plastic flying discs are destroyed quickly by their dogs, making an otherwise fun pastime an expensive outing. Flying discs made of annealed nylon are proven to last longer and thereby provide hours of enjoyable, affordable exercise for you and your dog.

Accommodations

Tug Toys

A tug toy is a hard rubber, cheap plastic, or polyurethane toy which allows a dog and his owner to have a game of tug-o-war. The owner grips one end while the dog grips the other—then they pull. The polyurethane flexible tug toy is the best on the market at the present time. Your pet shop will have one to show you. The polyurethane toys are clear in color and stay soft forever. Cheap plastic tug toys are indisputably dangerous, and the hard-rubber tug toys get brittle too fast and are too stiff for most dogs; however, there *is* a difference in price—just ask the advice of any shop operator.

Most every dog loves a challenging tug of war. Tug toys of sturdy polyurethane and strong cotton floss are favorites of many dogs.

Balls made of annealed nylon make fetching safe, pleasing and hygienic for your dog. Their virtually indestructible construction prevents the dog from tearing pieces of the ball and ingesting them, and the appealing scent inspires an enthusiastic retrieve. When worn, as shown here, nylon balls should be replaced with new ones.

Balls

Nobody has to tell you about playing ball with your dog. The reminder you may need is that you should not throw the ball where traffic might interfere with the dog's catching or fetching of it. The ball should not be cheap plastic (a dog's worst enemy as far as toys are concerned) but made of a substantial material. Balls made of nylon are practically indestructible, but they are very hard and must be rolled, never thrown. The same balls made of polyurethane are great—they bounce and are soft. The Nylabone® and Gumabone® balls are scented and flavored, and dogs can easily find them when lost.

Other manufacturers make balls of almost every substance, including plastic, cotton, and wood. Billiard balls, baseballs, tennis balls, and so on, have all been used by dog owners who want their dogs to play with them in a game of catch. A strong caveat is that you use only those balls made especially for dogs.

With the variety of safe, exercise-oriented chew products available, there is little excuse for a sedentary, plaque-infested existence to persist in an otherwise healthy dog.

Housebreaking and Training

Housebreaking can be the groundwork on which all future training is based. The two most commonly recommended methods involve paper training and crate training. When paper training is used, owners often employ litter boxes lined with paper to limit the area and make clean-up fast and easy.

HOUSEBREAKING

The new addition to your family may already have received some basic house training before his arrival in your home. If he has not, remember that a puppy will want to relieve himself about half a dozen times a day; it is up to you to specify where and when he should "do his business." Housebreaking is your first training concern and should begin the moment you bring the puppy home.

Ideally, puppies should be taken outdoors after meals, as a full stomach will exert pressure on the bladder and colon. What goes into the dog must eventually come out; the period after his meal is the most natural and appropriate time. When he eliminates, he should be praised, for this will increase the likelihood of the same thing happening after every meal. He should also be encouraged to use the same area and will probably be attracted to it after frequent use.

Some veterinarians maintain that a puppy can learn to urinate

Housebreaking and Training

and defecate on command, if properly trained. The advantage of this conditioning technique is that your pet will associate the act of elimination with a particular word of your choice rather than with a particular time or place which might not always be convenient or available. So whether you are visiting an unfamiliar place or don't want to go outside with your dog in sub-zero temperatures, he will still be able to relieve himself when he hears the specific command word. Elimination will occur after this "trigger" phrase or word sets up a conditioned reflex in the dog, who will eliminate anything contained in his bladder or bowel upon hearing it. The shorter the word, the more you can repeat it and imprint it on your dog's memory.

Your chosen command word should be given simultaneously with the sphincter opening events in order to achieve perfect and rapid conditioning. This is why it is important to familiarize yourself with the tell-tale signs preceding your puppy's elimination process. Then you will be prepared to say the word at the crucial moment. There is usually a sense of urgency on the dog's part; he may follow a sniffing and circling pattern which you will soon recognize. It is important to use the command in his usual area only when you know the puppy

can eliminate, i.e., when his stomach or bladder is full. He will soon learn to associate the act with the word. One word of advice, however, if you plan to try out this method: never use the puppy's name or any other word which he might frequently hear about the house—you can imagine the result!

Finally, remember that any training takes time. Such a conditioned response can be obtained with intensive practice with any normal, healthy dog over six weeks of age. Even Pavlov's salivating dogs required fifty repetitions before the desired response was achieved. Patience and persistence will eventually produce results—do not lose heart!

Indoors, sheets of newspapers can be used to cover the specific area where your dog should relieve himself. These should be placed some distance away from his sleeping and feeding area, as a puppy will not urinate or defecate where he eats. When the newspapers are changed, the bottom papers should be placed on top of the new ones in order to reinforce the purpose of the papers by scent as well as by sight. The puppy should be praised during or immediately after he has made use of this particular part of the room. Each positive reinforcement increases the possibility of his using that area again.

When he arrives, it is advisable to limit the puppy to one room, usually the kitchen, as it most likely has a linoleum or easily washable floor surface. Given the run of the house, the sheer size of the place will seem overwhelming and confusing and he might leave his "signature"

PATIENCE, PERSISTENCE, AND PRAISE

As with a human baby, you must be patient, tolerant, and understanding of your pet's mistakes, making him feel loved and wanted, not rejected and isolated. You wouldn't hit a baby for soiling his diapers, as you

An anchored lead can be the solution to a yard without a fence.

on your furniture or clothes! There will be time later to familiarize him gradually with his new surroundings.

would realize that he was not yet able to control his bowel movements; be as compassionate with your canine infant. Never rub his nose in his excreta. Never indulge in the common practice of punishing him with a rolled-up newspaper. Never hit a puppy with your hand. He will only become "hand-shy" and learn to fear you. Usually the punishment is meted out sometime after the offense and loses its efficacy, as the bewildered dog cannot connect the two events. Moreover, by association, he will soon learn to be afraid of you and anything to do with newspapers—including, perhaps, that area where he is *supposed* to relieve himself!

Most puppies are eager to please. Praise, encouragement, and reward (particularly the food

From the moment you bring your dog home, the rules of the house must be enforced to ensure a consistently obedient home companion.

variety) will produce far better results than any scolding or physical punishment. Moreover, it is far better to dissuade your puppy from doing certain things, such as chewing on chair legs or other furniture, by making those objects particularly distasteful to him. Some pet shops stock bitter apple sprays or citronella compounds for application to furniture legs. If these are ineffective, you could smear them with a generous amount of hot chili sauce or cayenne pepper mixed with petroleum jelly, for example. This would make it seem as if the object itself was administering the

Professionals cite that housebreaking on newspapers can cause some dogs to believe that it is always okay to excrete on papers, regardless of location. Housebreaking pads are used by many cautious owners.

punishment whenever he attempted to chew it. He probably wouldn't need a second reminder!

Remember that the reason a dog has housebreaking or behavior problems is because his owner has allowed them to develop. This is why you must begin as you intend to continue, letting your dog know what is acceptable and unacceptable behavior. It is also important that you be consistent in your demands; you cannot feed him

from the dining room table one day and then punish him when he begs for food from your dinner guests.

TRAINING

You will want the newest member of your family to be welcomed by everyone; this will not happen if he urinates in every room of the house or barks all night! He needs training in the correct forms of behavior in this new human world. You cannot expect your puppy to become the perfect pet overnight. He needs your help in his socialization process. Training greatly facilitates and enhances the relationship of the dog to his owner and to the rest of society. A successfully trained dog can

Housebreaking and Training

be taken anywhere and behave well with anyone. Indeed, it is that one crucial word—*training*—which can transform an aggressive animal into a peaceful, well-behaved pet. Now, how does this "transformation" take place?

Some owners of small dogs use a figure-eight-style harness as a means of restraint.

Collars should always be worn, with identification tag and license attached.

WHEN AND HOW TO TRAIN

Like housebreaking, training should begin as soon as the puppy enters the house. The formal training sessions should be short but frequent, for example, ten to fifteen minute periods three times a day. These are much more effective than long, tiring sessions of half an hour which might soon become boring. You are building your relationship with your puppy during these times, so make them as enjoyable as possible. It is a good idea to have these sessions *before* the puppy's meal, not after it when he wouldn't feel like exerting himself; the dog will then associate something pleasurable with his training sessions and look forward to them.

THE COLLAR AND LEASH

Your puppy should become used to a collar and leash as soon as possible. If he is very young, a thin, choke-chain collar can be used, but you will need a larger and heavier one for training when he is a little older. Remember to have his name and address on an identification tag attached to his collar, as you don't want to lose your pet if he

The variety of canine collars and leashes available surely allows for the personal touch.

A choke collar can be an effective training tool when used properly.

should happen to leave your premises and explore the neighborhood!

Let the puppy wear his collar until he is used to how it feels. After a short time he will soon become accustomed to it and you can attach the leash. He might resist your attempts to lead him or simply sit down and refuse to budge. Fight him for a few minutes, tugging on the leash if necessary, then let him relax for the day. He won't be trained until he learns that he must obey the pull under any circumstance, but this will take a few sessions. Remember that a dog's period of concentration is short, so LITTLE and OFTEN is the wisest course of action—and

patience is the password to success.

GIVING COMMANDS

When you begin giving your puppy simple commands, make them as short as possible and use the same word with the same meaning at all times, for example, "Heel," "Sit," and "Stay." You must be consistent; otherwise your puppy will become confused. The dog's name should prefix all commands to attract his attention. Do not become impatient with him however many times you have to repeat your command.

A good way to introduce the "Come" command is by calling the puppy when his meal is ready. Once this is learned, you can call your pet to you at will, always remembering to praise him for his prompt obedience. This "reward," or positive reinforcement, is such a crucial part of training that a Director of the New York Academy of Dog Training constructed his whole teaching program upon the methods of "Love, Praise, and Reward." Incidentally, if you use the command "Come," use it every time. Don't switch to "Come here" or "Come boy," as this will only confuse your dog.

It is worth underlining the fact that punishment is an ineffective teaching technique. We have already seen this in housebreaking. For example, if your pup should run away, it

A puppy's collar should be light and comfortable, yet still effectively secure the dog.

would be senseless to beat him when he eventually returns; he would only connect the punishment with his return, not with running away! In addition, it is unwise to call him to you to punish him, as he will soon learn not to respond when you call his name.

A lead that allows for a sure, comfortable grip is a training necessity. Introduce your new dog to the lead slowly. When he becomes comfortable with it, training can begin.

SOME SPECIFIC COMMANDS

"Sit" This is one of the easiest and most useful commands for your dog to learn, so it is a good idea to begin with it. The only equipment required is a leash, a collar, and a few tasty tidbits. Take your dog out for some exercise before his meal. After about five minutes, call him to you, praise him when he arrives,

A popular item with owners who love to walk their dogs is the harness. The harness fits comfortably around the dog's forequarters and displaces the pressure of the owner's tug on the lead.

and slip his collar on him. Hold the leash tightly in your right hand; this should force the dog's head up and focus his attention on you. As you say "Sit" in a loud, clear voice, with your left hand press steadily on his rump until he is in a sitting position. As soon as he is in the correct position, praise him and give him the tidbit you have in your hand. Now wait a few minutes to let him rest and repeat the routine. Through repetition, the dog soon associates the word with the act. Never make the lesson too long. Eventually your praise will be reward enough for your puppy. Other methods to teach this command exist, but this one, executed with care and moderation, has proven the most effective.

"Sit-Stay/Stay" To teach your pet to remain in one place or "stay" on your command, first of all order him to the sitting position at your side. Lower your left hand with the flat of your palm in front of his nose and your fingers pointing downwards. Hold the leash high and taut behind his head so that he cannot move. Speak the command "Sit-stay" and, as you are giving it, step in front of him. Repeat the command and tighten the leash so the animal cannot follow you. Walk completely around him, repeating the command and keeping him motionless by holding the leash at arm's length above him to check his movement. When he remains in this position for about fifteen seconds, you can begin the second part of the training. You will have to exchange the leash for a nylon cord or rope about twenty to thirty feet long. Repeat the whole routine from the beginning and be ready to prevent any movement towards you with a sharp "Sit-stay." Move around him in ever-widening circles until you are about fifteen feet away from him. If he still remains seated, you can pat yourself on the back! One useful thing to remember is that the dog makes associations with what you say, how you say it, and what you do while you are saying it. Give this command in a firm, clear tone of voice, perhaps using an admonishing forefinger raised, warning the dog to "stay."

Two training accessories especially common with obedience trial enthusiasts are the hurdle (above) and the dumbbell (below). To see dogs performing with these and other field accessories, attend an obedience competition. Remember that training requires consistency and commitment, but the rewards are well worth the effort.

"Heel" When you walk your dog, you should hold the leash firmly in your right hand. The dog should walk on your left so you have the leash crossing your body. This enables you to have greater control over the dog.

Let your dog lead you for the first few moments so that he fully understands that freedom can be his if he goes about it properly. He already knows that when he wants to go outdoors the leash and collar are necessary, so he has respect for the leash. Now, if he starts to pull in one direction while walking, all you do is *stop walking.* He will walk a few steps and then find that he can't walk any further. He will then turn and look into your face. *This is the crucial point!* Just stand there for a moment and stare right back at him . . . now walk another ten feet and stop again. Again your dog will probably walk to the end of the leash, find he can't go any further, and turn around and look again. If he starts to pull and jerk, just stand there. After he quiets down, bend down and comfort him, as he may be frightened. Keep up this training until he learns not to outwalk you.

Once the puppy obeys the pull of the leash, half of your training is accomplished. "Heeling" is a necessity for a well-behaved dog, so teach him to walk beside you, head even with your knee.

Nothing looks sadder than a big dog taking his helpless owner for a walk. It is annoying to passers-by and other dog owners to have a large dog, however friendly, bear down on them and entangle dogs, people, and packages.

To teach your dog, start off walking briskly, saying "Heel" in a firm voice. Pull back with a sharp jerk if he lunges ahead, and if he lags repeat the command and tug on the leash, not allowing him to drag behind. After the dog has learned to heel at various speeds on leash, you

The lead is an essential tool for teaching such commands as "heel," "come," and "down."

can remove it and practice heeling free, but have it ready to snap on again as soon as he wanders.

"Come" Your dog has already learned to come to you when you call his name. Why? Because you only call him when his food is ready or when you wish to play with him or praise him. Outdoors such a response is more difficult to achieve, if he is happily playing by himself or with other dogs, so he must be trained to come to you when he is called. To teach him to come, let him reach the end of a long lead, then give the command, gently pulling him towards you at the same time. As soon as he associates the word *come* with the action of moving towards you, pull only when he does not respond immediately. As he starts to come, move back to make him learn that he must come from a distance as well as when he is close to you. Soon you may be able to practice without a leash, but if he is slow to come or actively disobedient, go to him and pull him toward you, repeating the command. Always remember to reward his successful completion of a task.

"Down" Teaching the "down" command ideally begins while your dog is still a pup. During puppyhood your dog frequently will lie down, as this position is one of the dog's most natural positions. Invest some time, and keep close watch over your pup. Each time he begins to lie, repeat in a low convincing tone the word "down." If for the first day of training, you concur a majority of the dog's sitting with your commands and continue with reinforcement and moderate praise your pup should conquer the "down" command in no time.

Teaching the "down" command to a mature dog likely will require more effort. Although the lying position is still natural to a dog, his being forced into it is not. Some dogs may react with fear, anger, or confusion. Others may accept the process and prove quick learners. Have your

For the dog that responds with anger or aggression, attach a lead (and a muzzle) and have the dog sit facing you at a close distance. There should be a J-loop formed by the lead. With moderate force, relative to the size and strength of your dog, step on the J-loop, forcing the dog down, while repeating the command "down" in a low forceful tone. When the dog is down, moderate praise should

Threats and physical punishment have no place in the canine training process. The keys to effective training are patience, persistence, and praise.

dog sit and face you. If he is responsive and congenial, gently take his paws, and slowly pull them towards you; give the "down" command as he approaches the proper position. Repeat several times: moderate reinforcement of this procedure should prove rewardingly successful.

be given. If the dog proves responsive, you may attempt extending his legs to the "down" position—leaving the muzzle on, of course. Daily reinforcement of the training method will soon yield the desired results. The keys to remember are: patience, persistence, and praise.

Behavior Modification

"Problems with the Barking Dog" and "Aggressive Behavior and Dominance" are extracts from the veterinary monograph *Canine Behavior* (a compilation of columns from *Canine Practice,* a journal published by Veterinary Practice Publishing Company).

PROBLEMS WITH THE BARKING DOG

One of the most frequent complaints about canine behavior is barking. Aside from the biting dog, the barking dog is probably the pet peeve of many non-dog owners. I know of at least one city in which owners of dogs that bark excessively, and for which there are complaints on file, are required to take steps to eliminate the barking.

Canine practitioners are drawn into problems with barking when they are asked for their advice in helping an owner come up with a solution or, as a last resort, when they are requested to perform a debarking operation or even euthanasia. In this column I will deal with some of the factors that apparently cause dogs to bark and suggest some corrective approaches.

Barking is, of course, a natural response for many dogs. They have an inherited predisposition to bark as an alarm when other dogs or people approach their territory. Alarm barking makes

A problem facing many dog owners is excessive vocalization. Fortunately, a number of correctives have proven successful.

many dogs valuable as household watchdogs and is not necessarily undesirable behavior. With a different vocal tone and pattern, dogs bark when they are playing with each other. On occasion dogs have a tendency to bark back at other dogs or join in with other barking dogs.

In addition to inherited barking tendencies, dogs can also learn to bark if the barking is followed, at least sometimes, by a reward. Thus dogs may bark when they wish to come in the house or to get out of a kennel. Some dogs are trained to bark upon hearing the command "speak" for a food reward.

One of the first approaches to

Behavior Modification

take when discussing a barking problem is to determine if the behavior is a manifestation of a natural (inherited) tendency or is learned behavior which has been rewarded in the past.

Can Barking Be Extinguished?
Extinction, as a way of eliminating a behavioral problem, may be considered when it is clear that the behavior has been learned and when one can identify the specific rewarding or reinforcing factors that maintain the behavior.

For example, the dog that barks upon hearing the command "speak" is periodically rewarded with food and praise. If a dog is never, ever given food or praise again when it barks after being told to "speak," it will eventually stop this type of barking. This is the process of extinction and it implies that the

Reward in the form of treats is often effective.

behavior must be repeated but never again rewarded.

A more practical example of the possible use of extinction would be in dealing with the dog that apparently barks because, at least occasionally, it is allowed in the house. By not allowing the dog in the house until the barking has become very frequent and loud, the owners may have shaped the barking behavior to that which is the most objectionable. If the dog is never allowed in the house again when barking, the barking should eventually be extinguished—at least theoretically.

How Should Punishment Be Used? Sometimes it is not feasible to attempt to extinguish barking even if it seems to be the case that the behavior was learned. This brings up the advisability of punishment. Clients who seek advice in dealing with a barking problem may already have employed some type of punishment such as shouting at the dog or throwing something at it. That this type of punishment is ineffective is attested to by the fact that the client is seeking advice. By shouting at a dog or hitting, a person interferes with what effect the punishment may have on the behavior itself through the arousal of autonomic reactions and escape attempts or submissive responses by the dog.

102

The Water Bucket Approach

I am rather impressed by the ingenuity of some dog owners in coming up with ways to punish a dog for barking without being directly involved in administering the punishment. One such harried dog owner I talked to, who was also a veterinarian, was plagued by his dog's barking in the kennel commencing at about 1:30 a.m. every night. A platform to hold a bucket of water was constructed over the area of the kennel in which the dog usually chose to bark. Through a system of hinges, ropes, and pulleys, a mechanism was devised so that the dog owner could pull a rope from his bedroom window, dumping a bucket of water on the dog when he started to bark. The bucket was suspended such that once it was dumped, it uprighted itself and the owner could fill it again remotely by turning on a garden hose. After two appropriate dunkings, the dog's barking behavior was apparently eliminated.

With a little ingenuity, a bucket attached to a trap door can be constructed. Soaking the dog in this surprising manner can possibly extinguish a bad barking habit. Always take into consideration the weather conditions, the health and age of your dog, and the cause of the barking problem before embarking on the water-bucket cure.

In advising a client on the type of punishment discussed above, keep in mind one important consideration. From the time the owner is ready to administer punishment for barking, every attempt should be made to punish all undesirable barking from that point on and not to allow excessively long periods of barking to go unpunished. Thus it may be necessary to keep a dog indoors when away unless the dog will be punished for barking when the owner is gone.

Alternative Responses Barking dogs are, and probably always will be, one of the enduring problems of dog owners. Barking is relatively effortless, and it is such a natural response for many dogs that it is admittedly hard to eliminate with either punishment or a program of conditioning non-barking. In some instances it may be advisable to forget about eliminating barking and to suggest that the problem be dealt with by changing the circumstances which lead to barking. For example, a dog that barks continuously in the backyard while the owners are away may not bark if left in the house while they are gone. But the problem of keeping the dog in the house may be related to inadequate house training or the dog's shedding hair or climbing onto the furniture. It may be easier to correct these latter behavioral problems than it is to change the barking behavior.

Especially for aggressive dogs, muzzles can prevent both injuries and lawsuits.

AGGRESSIVE BEHAVIOR AND DOMINANCE

Aggressiveness can have many causes. Determining what kind of aggression an animal is manifesting is a prerequisite to successful treatment of the behavior. A frequent problem that is presented to the practitioner is one of aggression related to dominance.

Dogs, which are social animals, have a hierarchal system of dominance within their pack. This predisposition to take a dominant or submissive position relative to fellow canines also occurs in relationship to people. Only in unusual situations would a submissive dog threaten a dominant animal, and almost never would it physically assault its superior. The dominant dog, however, frequently threatens submissive individuals to maintain its position. In a household setting, a person may be the object of threats, and when the person backs off, the dog's position is reassured. The aggressive behavior is also reinforced, and when behavior is reinforced it is likely to recur.

Case History The following is a typical case history of a dog presented for aggression stemming from dominance.

Max was a two-year-old intact male Cocker Spaniel. He had been acquired by Mr. Smith, one year prior to his owner's marriage, as a puppy. He liked and was well liked by both Mr. and Mrs. Smith. He frequently solicited and received attention from both people. However, several times over the last few months, Max had snapped at Mrs. Smith and repeatedly growled at her. A detailed anamnesis revealed that such incidents usually occurred in situations where the dog wanted his own way or did not want to be bothered. He would growl if asked to move off a chair or if persistently commanded to do a specific task. He growled if Mrs. Smith came between him and a young female Cocker Spaniel acquired a year ago. He also refused to let Mrs. Smith take anything from his possession.

Behavior Modification

Max never showed any of these aggressive behaviors toward Mr. Smith or strangers. Admittedly he did not have much opportunity to demonstrate such behaviors toward strangers. A description of the dog's body and facial postures and circumstances under which the

Dogs can become possessive of their playthings or aggressive in defense of their territory.

aggression occurred did not indicate that this was a case of fear-induced aggression, but rather one of assertion of dominance.

Mrs. Smith's reaction to the aggression was always to retreat, and, hence, the dog was rewarded for his assertiveness. She had never physically disciplined the dog and was afraid to do so. To encourage her to physically take control of the dog would likely have resulted in her being bitten. The dominance-submissive relationship had to be reversed in a more subtle manner.

Instructions to Client Mrs. Smith was instructed to avoid all situations which might evoke any aggressive signs from Max. This was to prevent any further reinforcement of his growling and threats.

Both she and her husband were not to indiscriminately pet or show affection towards the dog. For the time being, if Max solicited attention from Mr. Smith, he was to ignore the dog. Mrs. Smith was to take advantage of Max's desire for attention by giving him a command which he had to obey before she praised and petted him. She was also to take advantage of high motivation levels for other activities whenever such situations arose. Max had to obey a command before she gave him anything—

before she petted him, before she let him out or in, etc.

Mrs. Smith also was to assume total care of the dog and become "the source of all good things in life" for Max. She was to feed him, take him on walks, play with him, etc.

Mrs. Smith also spent 5–10 minutes a day teaching Max simple parlor tricks and obedience responses for coveted food rewards as well as praise. These were entirely fun and play sessions—but within a few days the dog had acquired the habit of quickly responding to commands. And this habit transferred over to the non-game situations.

Results Within a few weeks,

The dog's bed can become an object of possession. The dog can come to perceive it as his territory, not allowing others to come near. In such instances behavior modification may be necessary.

Max had ceased to growl and threaten Mrs. Smith in situations that he previously had. He would move out of her way or lie quietly when she would pass by him. She could order him off the furniture and handle the female Cocker Spaniel without eliciting threats from Max.

Mrs. Smith still felt that she would not be able to take the objects from Max's possession. Additional instructions were

Behavior Modification

A dog comes to associate the pleasure of receiving a treat with the action immediately preceding it. Treats are effective in shaping behavior and building a relationship with your pet when they are used judiciously and in moderation.

given to her. She then began placing a series of objects at progressively closer distances to the dog while the dog was in a sit-stay position. After she placed the object on the floor for a short time, she would pick it up. If the dog was still in a sit-stay (which it always was), he received a reward of cheese and verbal praise. Eventually the objects were to be placed and

removed from directly in front of the dog. At first she was to use objects that the dog did not care much about and then progressively use more coveted items. This was what she was supposed to do, but before she actually had completed the program she called in excitedly to report that she had taken a piece of stolen food and a household ornament from Max's mouth. And he didn't even object! She said she had calmly told Max to sit. He did. He was so used to doing so, in the game and other situations, that the response was now automatic. She walked over, removed the item from his mouth, and praised him.

Mrs. Smith did resume the systematic presentation of objects and put the dog on an intermittent schedule of food and praise reinforcement during the practice sessions. Mr. Smith again began interacting with Max.

A progress check six months later indicated Max was still an obedient dog and had definitely assumed a submissive position relative to both of his owners. The dominance hierarchy between Max and Mrs. Smith had been reversed *without resorting to any physical punishment.* Mrs. Smith was instructed to reinforce her dominance position by frequently giving Max a command and reinforcing him for the appropriate response.

Summary The essential elements in treatment of such cases are as follows. First, of course, there must be a correct diagnosis of what kind of aggressive behavior is occurring. During the course of treatment, the submissive person(s) should avoid all situations that might evoke an aggressive attitude by the dog. All other family members should totally ignore the dog during the treatment interim. The person most dominated by the dog should take over complete care of the dog in addition to spending 5–10 minutes a day teaching the dog tricks or simple obedience commands (sit-stay is a useful one to gain control of the dog in subsequent circumstances). These should be fun-and-games situations. Food rewards are highly recommended in addition to simple praise.

The person submissive to the dog should take the opportunity to give the dog a command, which must be obeyed, before doing anything pleasant for the dog.

It must be emphasized to the owner that no guarantee can be made that the dog will never threaten or be aggressive again. What is being done, as with all other aggression cases, is an attempt to reduce the likelihood, incidence, and intensity of occurrence of the aggressive behavior.

DESTRUCTIVE TENDENCIES

It is ironical but true that a dog's destructive behavior in the home may be proof of his love for his owner. He may be trying to get more attention from his owner or, in other cases, may be expressing his frustration at his owner's absence. An abundance

Some crates have wire-mesh fronts while others do not. The primary consideration in choosing a crate is its ventilation.

of unused energy may also contribute to a dog's destructive behavior, and therefore the owner should ensure that his dog has, at least, twenty minutes of vigorous exercise a day.

As a dog's destructive tendencies may stem from his desire to get more attention from his owner, the latter should devote specific periods each day to his dog when he is actively interacting with him. Such a period should contain practice obedience techniques during which the owner can reward the dog with his favorite food as well as praise and affection.

Planned departure conditioning is one specific technique which has been used to solve the problem of destructive tendencies in a puppy. It eventually ensures the dog's good behavior during the owner's absence. A series of

Not just great recreational devices to channel doggie tensions, the Gumabone® products have been scientifically proven to reduce tartar and plaque build-up. These products are available in many shapes and sizes. Gumabone® products should be replaced regularly when they become excessively worn.

short departures, which are identical to real departures, should condition the dog to behave well in the owner's absence. How is this to be achieved? Initially, the departures are so short (2–5 minutes) that the dog has no opportunity to be destructive. The dog is always rewarded for having been good when the owner returns. Gradually the duration of the departures is increased. The departure time is also varied so that the dog does not know when the owner is going to return. Since a different kind of behavior is now expected, it is best if a new stimulus or "atmosphere" is introduced into the training sessions to permit the dog to distinguish these departures as different from previous departures when he was destructive.

This new stimulus could be the sound of the radio or television. The association which the dog will develop is that whenever the "signal" or "stimulus" is on, the owner will return in an unknown

A proven safe chew product.

A safe tug toy.

period of time and, if the dog has not been destructive, he will be rewarded. As with the daily owner-dog interaction, the food reward is especially useful.

If the dog misbehaves during his owner's absence, the owner should speak sternly to him and isolate him from social contact for at least thirty minutes. (Puppies hate to be ignored.) Then the owner should conduct another departure of a shorter time and generously reward good behavior when he returns. The owner should progress slowly enough in the program so that once the departure has been initiated, the dog is never given an opportunity to make a mistake.

If planned departures are working satisfactorily, the departure time may gradually be extended to several hours. To reduce the dog's anxiety when left alone, he should be given a "safety valve" such as the indestructible Nylabone® to play with and chew on.

Health Care

From the moment you purchase your puppy, the most important person in both your lives becomes your veterinarian. His professional advice and treatment will ensure the good health of your pet. The vet is the first person to call when illness or accidents occur. Do *not* try to be your own veterinarian or apply human remedies to canine diseases. However, just as you would keep a first aid kit handy for minor injuries sustained by members of your family at home, so you should keep a similar kit prepared for your pet.

First aid for your dog would consist of stopping any bleeding, cleaning the wound, and

Even in your own back yard, injuries can occur.

preventing infection. Thus your kit might contain medicated powder, gauze bandages, and adhesive tape to be used in case of cuts. If the cut is deep and bleeding profusely, the bandage should be applied very tightly to help in the formation of a clot. A tight bandage should not be kept in place longer than necessary, so take your pet to the veterinarian immediately.

Walking or running on a cut pad prevents the cut from healing. Proper suturing of the cut and regular changing of the bandages should have your pet's wound healed in a week to ten days. A minor cut should be covered with a light bandage, for you want as much air as possible to reach the wound. Do not apply wads of cotton to a wound; they will stick to the area and may cause contamination.

You should also keep some hydrogen peroxide available, as it is useful in cleaning wounds and is also one of the best and simplest emetics known. Cotton applicator swabs are useful for applying ointment or removing debris from the eyes. A pair of tweezers should also be kept handy for removing foreign bodies from the dog's neck, head or body.

Nearly everything a dog might contract in the way of sickness has basically the same set of symptoms: loss of appetite, diarrhea, dull eyes, dull coat,

When emergencies occur, it pays to be prepared. A first-aid kit, well stocked with common sense medical accessories and tools, is helpful to have available at all times.

warm and/or runny nose, and a high temperature. Therefore, it is most important to take his temperature at the first sign of illness. To do this, you will need a rectal thermometer which should be lubricated with petroleum jelly. Carefully insert it into the rectum, holding it in place for at least two minutes. It must be held firmly; otherwise there is the danger of its being sucked up into the rectum or slipping out, thus giving an inaccurate reading. The normal temperature for a dog is between 101° and 102.5°F. If your pet is seriously ill or injured in an accident, your veterinarian will advise you what to do before he arrives.

SWALLOWING FOREIGN OBJECTS

Most of us have had experience with a child swallowing a foreign object. Usually it is a small coin; occasionally it may be a fruit pit or something more dangerous. Dogs, *as a general rule,* will not swallow anything which isn't edible. There are, however, many dogs that swallow pebbles or small shiny objects such as pins, coins, and bits of cloth and plastic. This is especially true of dogs that are offered so-called "chew toys."

Chew toys are available in many sizes, shapes, colors and materials. Some even have whistles which sound when the dog's owner plays with it or when the dog chomps on it quickly. Most dogs attack the whistle first, doing everything possible to make it stop squeaking. Obviously, if the whistle is made of metal, a dog can injure its mouth, teeth, or tongue. Therefore, *never* buy a "squeak toy" made with a metal whistle.

Other chew toys are made of vinyl, a cheap plastic which is soft to the touch and pliable. Most of the cute little toys that are figures of animals or people are made of this cheap plastic. They are sometimes hand-painted in countries where the cost of such labor is low. Not only is the paint used dangerous to dogs, because of the lead content, but the vinyl tears easily and is usually destroyed by the dog during the first hour. Small bits of vinyl may be ingested and cause blockage of the intestines. You are, therefore, reminded of these things before you buy anything vinyl for your dog!

Very inexpensive dog toys, usually found in supermarkets and other low-price venues, may be made of polyethylene. These are to be avoided completely, as this cheap plastic is, for some odd reason, attractive to dogs. Dogs destroy the toy in minutes and sometimes swallow the indigestible bits and pieces that come off. Most pet shops carry only safe toys.

WHAT TOYS ARE SAFE FOR DOGS?

Hard Rubber Toys made of hard rubber are usually safe for dogs, providing the toy is made of 100% hard rubber and not a compound of rubber and other materials. The rubber must be "virgin" and not re-ground from old tires, tubes, and other scrap rubber products. The main problem with rubber, even 100% virgin rubber, is that it oxidizes quickly, especially when subjected to the ultraviolet rays of the sun and a dog's saliva. The rubber then tends to be brittle, to crack, to dust off, and to be extremely dangerous to dogs that like swallowing things.

From top to bottom, *the four common bite types are: (a) level, (b) scissors, (c) undershot, and (d) overshot. Different breeds have different bite types and one bite type may be desirable in your breed and most undesirable in another.*

Nylon Toys Toys made of nylon could well be the safest of all toys, *providing the nylon is annealed.* Nylon that is not annealed is very fragile ,and if you smash it against a hard surface, it might shatter like glass. The same is true when the weather is cold and the nylon drops below freezing. Thus far there is only one line of dog toys that is made of annealed virgin nylon—Nylabone®. These toys are not only annealed but they are flavored and scented. The flavors and scents, such as hambone, are undetectable by humans, but dogs seem to find them attractive.

Some nylon bones have the flavor sprayed on them or molded into them. These cheaper bones are easy to detect—just smell them. If you discern an odor, you know they are poorly made. The main

The inherent need to chew is strong in dogs of all ages. The canine's constant chewing of his favorite chew products will necessitate their regular replacement. When a bone becomes frayed, it's time to replace it.

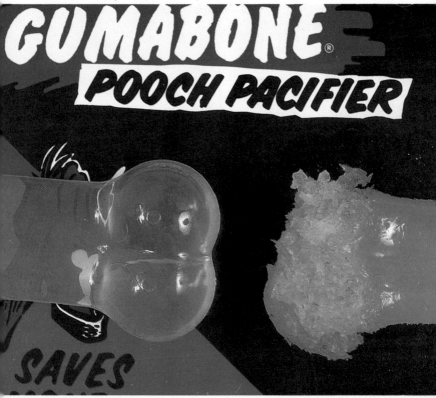

problem with the nylon toys that have an odor is that they are not annealed and they "smell up" the house or car. The dog's saliva dilutes the odor of the bone, and when he drops it on your rug, this odor attaches itself to the rug and is quite difficult to remove.

Annealed nylon may be the best there is ,but it is not 100% safe. The Nylabone® dog chews are really meant to be Pooch Pacifiers®. This trade name indicates the effect intended for the dog, which is to relieve the tension in your excited puppy or adult dog who is left alone or wants to "spite" you. Instead of chewing up the furniture or some other object, he chews up his Nylabone® instead. Many dogs ignore the Nylabone® for weeks, suddenly attacking it when they have to relieve their doggie tensions.

Some dogs may have jaws strong enough to chomp off a piece of Nylabone®, but this is extremely rare. *One word of caution:* the Nylabone® should be replaced when the dog has chewed down the knuckle. Most dogs slowly scrape off small slivers of nylon which pass harmlessly through their digestive tract. The resultant frizzled bone actually becomes a toothbrush.

One of the great characteristics of nylon bones is that they can be boiled and

The Gumaknot® is the favorite chew item of many dogs.

Above: *The Nylabone® is an effective, proven-safe therapeutic device.* ***Below***: *The Gumaball® is useful for outside recreation, exercise, and tooth care.*

Doggie treats come in a wide variety of sizes, shapes, and flavors. While they can be useful as rewards and occasional tidbits, they do not satisfy the dog's need to chew. Treats are best used for what they are intended—as treats.

sterilized. If a dog loses interest in his Nylabone®, or it is too hard for him to chew due to his age and the condition of his teeth, you can cook it in some chicken or beef broth, allowing it to boil for 30 minutes. Let it cool down normally. It will then be perfectly sterile and re-flavored for the next dog. *Don't try this with plastic bones, as they will melt and ruin your pot.*

Polyurethane Toys Toys made of polyurethane are almost as good as nylon bones—but not quite. There are several brands on the market: ignore the ones which have scents that you can discern. Some of the scented polyurethane bones have an unbearable odor after the scent has rubbed off the bone and onto your rug or car seat. Again, look for the better-quality polyurethane toy. Gumabone® is

a flexible material, the same as used for making artificial hearts and the bumpers on automobiles, thus it is strong and stable. It is not as strong as Nylabone®, but many dogs like it because it is soft.

The most popular of the Gumabone® products made in polyurethane are the tug toys, balls, and Frisbee® flying discs. These items are almost clear in color, have the decided advantage of lasting a long time, and are useful in providing exercise for both a dog and his master or mistress.

Whatever dog toy you buy, be sure it is high quality. Pet shops, as a rule, carry the better-quality toys, while supermarkets seem to be concerned only with price. Of course there may be exceptions, but you are best advised to ask your local pet shop operator—or even your veterinarian—what toys are suitable for *your* dog.

In conclusion, if your dog is a swallower of foreign objects, don't give him anything cheap to chew on. If he swallows a coin, you can hardly blame the Treasury! Unless your dog is carefully supervised, use only the largest size Nylabone®, and replace it as soon as the dog chews down the knuckles. *Do not let the dog take the Nylabone® outdoors.* First of all he can hide and bury it, digging it up when his tensions rise. Then, too, all nylon becomes more brittle when it freezes, even Nylabone®.

IF YOUR PET SWALLOWS POISON

A poisoned dog must be treated instantly; any delay could cause his death. Different poisons act in different ways and require different treatments. If you know the dog has swallowed an acid, alkali, gasoline, or kerosene, do not induce vomiting. Give milk to dilute the poison and rush him to the vet. If you can find the bottle or container of poison, check the label to see if there is a recommended antidote. If not, try to induce vomiting by giving him a mixture of hydrogen peroxide and water. Mix the regular drugstore strength of hydrogen peroxide (3%) with an equal part of water, but do not attempt to pour it down your dog's throat, as that could cause inhalation pneumonia. Instead, simply pull the dog's lips away from the side of his mouth, making a pocket for depositing the liquid. Use at least a tablespoonful of the mixture for every ten pounds of your dog's

Handling a dog who is sick or injured requires skill. To protect yourself from being bitten, you should first secure the dog's muzzle with a slow, cautious motion, if no safety muzzle is available. Then the animal can be treated or transported as required.

weight. He will vomit in about two minutes. When his stomach has settled, give him a teaspoonful of Epsom salts in a little water to empty the intestine quickly. The hydrogen peroxide, on ingestion, becomes oxygen and water and is harmless to your dog; it is the best antidote for phosphorus, which is often used in rat poisons. After you have administered this emergency treatment to your pet and his stomach and bowels have been emptied, rush him to your veterinarian for further care.

DANGER IN THE HOME

There are numerous household products that can prove fatal if ingested by your pet. These include rat poison, antifreeze, boric acid, hand soap, detergents, insecticides, mothballs, household cleansers,

Water hemlock is one of the many poisonous plants that can cause serious complications if ingested by a canine.

bleaches, de-icers, polishes and disinfectants, paint and varnish removers, acetone, turpentine, and even health and beauty aids if ingested in large enough quantities. A word to the wise should be sufficient: what you would keep locked away from your two-year-old child should also be kept hidden from your pet.

There is another danger lurking within the home among the household plants, which are almost all poisonous, even if swallowed in small quantities. There are hundreds of poisonous plants around us, among which are: ivy leaves, cyclamen, lily of the valley, rhododendrons, tulip bulbs, azalea, wisteria, poinsettia

Suburban backyards are often fertile grounds for a variety of flowering plant types. Many of these pretty-to-the-eye plants can be harmful to a canine. Lily-of-the-valley is attractive and popular in some climates; it is, however, poisonous if ingested and should not be cultivated near the dog's living area.

Lactrodectus mactans, *better known as the black widow spider, is said to possess venom over 15 times as toxic as many rattlesnakes'. This spider most commonly occurs in warm climates. Owners are encouraged to inspect the dog's living area periodically for such lethal inhabitants.*

leaves, mistletoe, daffodils, delphiniums, foxglove leaves, the jimson weed—we cannot name them all. Rhubarb leaves, for example, either raw or cooked, can cause death or violent convulsions. Peach, elderberry, and cherry trees can cause cyanide poisoning if their bark is consumed.

There are also many insects that can be poisonous to dogs such as spiders, bees, wasps, and some flies. A few toads and frogs exude a fluid that can make a dog foam at the mouth—and even kill him—if he bites too hard!

There have been cases of dogs suffering nicotine poisoning by consuming the contents of full ashtrays which thoughtless smokers have left on the coffee table. Also, do not leave nails, staples, pins, or other sharp objects lying around. Likewise, don't let your puppy play with plastic bags which could suffocate him. Unplug, remove, or cover any electrical cords or wires near your dog. Chewing live wires could lead to severe mouth burns or death. Remember that an ounce of prevention is worth a pound of cure: keep all potentially dangerous objects out of your pet's reach.

Health Care

Bufo marinus, *the giant toad, is a very large species of toad that, when provoked, will produce a secretion that is toxic if ingested. The giant toad can potentially be a canine killer.*

VEHICLE TRAVEL SAFETY

A dog should never be left alone in a car. It takes only a few minutes for the heat to become unbearable in the summer, and to drop to freezing in the winter.

A dog traveling in a car or truck should be well behaved. An undisciplined dog can be deadly in a moving vehicle. The dog should be trained to lie on the back seat of the vehicle. Allowing your dog to stick its head out of the window is unwise. The dog may jump or it may get something in its eye. Some manufacturers sell seat belts and car seats designed for dogs.

Traveling with your dog in the back of your pick-up truck is an unacceptable notion and dangerous to all involved.

PROTECT YOURSELF FIRST

In almost all first aid situations, the dog is in pain. He may indeed be in shock and not appear to be suffering, until you move him. Then he may bite your hand or resist being helped at all. So if you want to help your dog, help yourself first by tying his mouth closed. To do this, use a piece of strong cloth four inches wide and three feet long, depending on the size of the dog. Make a loop in the middle of the strip and slip it over his nose with the knot under his chin and over the bony part of his nose.

Pull it tight and bring the ends back around his head behind the ears and tie it tightly, ending with a bow knot for quick, easy release. Now you can handle the dog safely. As a dog perspires through his tongue, do not leave the "emergency muzzle" on any longer than necessary.

ADMINISTERING MEDICINE

When you are giving liquid medicine to your dog, it is a good idea to pull the lips away from the side of the mouth, form a lip pocket, and let the liquid trickle past the tongue. Remain at his side, never in front of the dog, as he may cough and spray you with the liquid. Moreover, you must never pour liquid medicine while the victim's tongue is drawn out, as inhalation pneumonia could be the disastrous result.

Medicine in pill form is best administered by forcing the dog's mouth open, holding his head back, and placing the capsule as far back on his tongue as you can reach. To do this: put the palm of your hand over the dog's muzzle (his foreface) with your fingers on one side of his jaw, your thumb

An injured dog can bite, rather unintentionally. A make-shift muzzle can be used in the case of an emergency. A tie or a torn piece of cloth can suffice.

To avoid inhalation pneumonia, a syringe placed between the dog's gums can be used when administering liquid medications.

on the other. Press his lips hard against his teeth while using your other hand to pull down his lower jaw. With your two fingers, try to put the pill as far back on the dog's tongue as you can reach. Keep his mouth and nostrils closed and he should be forced to swallow the medicine. As the dog will not be feeling well, stroke his neck to comfort him and to help him swallow his medicine more easily. Do keep an eye on him for a few moments afterward, however, to make certain that he does not spit it out.

IN CASE OF AN ACCIDENT

It is often difficult for you to assess the dog's injuries after a road accident. He may appear normal, but there might be internal hemorrhaging. A vital organ could be damaged or ribs broken. Keep the dog as quiet and warm as possible; cover him with blankets or your coat to let his own body heat build up. Signs of shock are a rapid and weak pulse, glassy-eyed appearance, subnormal temperature, and slow capillary refill time. To determine the last symptom, press firmly against the dog's gums until they turn white. Release and count the number of seconds until the gums return to their normal color. If it is more than 2–3 seconds, the dog may be going into shock. Failure to return to the reddish pink color indicates that the dog may be in serious trouble and needs immediate assistance.

If artificial respiration is required, first open the dog's mouth and check for obstructions; extend his tongue and examine the pharynx. Clear his mouth of mucus and blood and hold the mouth slightly open. Mouth-to-mouth resuscitation involves holding the dog's tongue to the bottom of his mouth with one hand and sealing his nostrils with the other while you blow into his mouth. Watch for his chest to rise with each inflation. Repeat every 5–6 seconds, the equivalent of 10–12 breaths a minute.

If the veterinarian cannot come to you, try to improvise a stretcher to take the dog to him.

To administer pills, simply press the dog's lips against his teeth until he opens his mouth. Then place the pill as far back on the tongue as possible. Now hold the dog's mouth closed and see that the dog has swallowed. Praise him for his cooperation.

Health Care

To carry a puppy, wrap him in a blanket that has been folded into several thicknesses. If he is in shock, it is better to pick him up by holding one hand under his chest, the other under the hindquarters. This will keep him stretched out.

It is always better to roll an injured dog than to try and lift him. If you find him lying beside the road after a car accident, apply a muzzle even if you have to use someone's necktie to make one. Send someone for a blanket and roll him gently onto

it. Two people, one on each side, can make a stretcher out of the blanket and move the dog easily.

If no blanket is available and the injured dog must be moved, try to keep him as flat as possible. So many dogs' backs are broken in car accidents that one must first consider that possibility. However, if he can move his hind legs or tail, his spine is probably not broken. Get medical assistance for him immediately.

It should be mentioned that unfortunate car accidents, which can maim or kill your dog, can be avoided if he is confined at all times either indoors or, if out-of-doors, in a fenced-in yard or

Known as Elizabethan collars, these devices can be purchased at a pet store or provided by your veterinarian to prevent the dog from complications resulting from excessive licking or chewing.

Nightshade (left) and larkspur (right) are two plants that are poisonous when ingested. Many dogs eat small amounts of wild grass, which is often harmless if not sprayed with pesticides; however, the owner must be cautious that poisonous plants are not growing in the grass, for they can be accidentally consumed.

some other protective enclosure. *Never* allow your dog to roam free; even a well-trained dog may, for some unknown reason, dart into the street—and the result could be tragic.

If you need to walk your dog, leash him first so that he will be protected from moving vehicles.

PROTECTING YOUR PET

It is important to watch for any tell-tale signs of illness so that you can spare your pet any unnecessary suffering. Your dog's eyes, for example, should normally be bright and alert, so if the haw is bloodshot or partially covers the eye, it may be a sign of illness or irritation. If your dog has matter in the corners of his eyes, bathe them with a mild eye

wash; obtain ointment or eye drops from your veterinarian to treat a chronic condition.

If your dog seems to have something wrong with his ears which causes him to scratch at them or shake his head, cautiously probe the ear with a cotton swab. An accumulation of wax will probably work itself out. Dirt or dried blood, however, is indicative of ear mites or infection and should be treated immediately. Sore ears in the summer, due to insect bites, should be washed with mild soap and water, then covered with a soothing ointment and wrapped in gauze if necessary. Keep your pet away from insects until his ears heal, even if this means confining him indoors.

INOCULATIONS

Periodic check-ups by your veterinarian throughout your puppy's life are good health insurance. The person from whom your puppy was purchased should tell you what inoculations your puppy has had and when the next visit to the vet is necessary. You must make certain that your puppy has been vaccinated against the following infectious canine diseases: distemper, canine hepatitis, leptospirosis, rabies, parvovirus, and parainfluenza. Annual "boosters" thereafter provide inexpensive protection for your dog against such serious diseases. Puppies should also be checked for worms at an early age.

DISTEMPER

Young dogs are most susceptible to distemper, although it may affect dogs of all ages. Some signs of the disease are loss of appetite, depression, chills, and fever, as well as a watery discharge from the eyes and nose. Unless treated promptly, the disease goes into advanced stages with infections of the lungs, intestines, and nervous system. Dogs that recover may be impaired with paralysis, convulsions, a twitch, or some other defect, usually spastic in nature. Early inoculations in puppyhood

While the vet is inspecting your dog, secure him around the base of his neck and the tuck of his abdomen.

When a dog's ear is injured, it should be bandaged by a professional. A protective collar should then be secured.

should be followed by an annual booster to help protect against this disease.

CANINE HEPATITIS

The signs of hepatitis are drowsiness, vomiting, loss of appetite, high temperature, and great thirst. These signs may be accompanied by swellings of the head, neck, and abdomen. Vomiting may also occur. This disease strikes quickly, and death may occur in only a few hours. An annual booster shot is needed after the initial series of puppy shots.

LEPTOSPIROSIS

Infection caused by either of two serovars, *canicola* or *copehageni* is usually begun by the dog's licking substances contaminated by the urine or feces of infected animals. Brown rats are the main carriers of *copehageni*. The signs are weakness, vomiting, and a yellowish discoloration of the jaws, teeth, and tongue, caused by an inflammation of the kidneys. A veterinarian can administer the bacterins to protect your dog from this disease. The frequency of the doses is determined by the risk factor involved.

RABIES

This disease of the dog's central nervous system spreads by infectious saliva, which is transmitted by the bite of an infected animal. Of the two main classes of signs, the first is "furious rabies," in which the dog shows a period of melancholy or depression, then irritation, and finally paralysis. The first period can be from a few hours to several days, and during this time the dog is cross and will change his position often, lose his appetite, begin to lick, and bite or swallow foreign objects. During this phase the dog is spasmodically wild and has impulses to run away. The dog acts fearless and bites everything in sight. If he is caged or confined, he will fight at the bars and possibly break teeth or fracture his jaw. His bark becomes a peculiar howl. In the final stage, the animal's lower jaw becomes paralyzed and hangs down. He then walks with a stagger, and saliva drips from his mouth. About four to eight days after the onset of paralysis, the dog dies.

The second class of symptoms is referred to as "dumb rabies" and is characterized by the dog's walking in a bearlike manner with his head down. The lower jaw is paralyzed and the dog is unable to bite. It appears as if he has a bone caught in his throat.

If a dog is bitten by a rabid animal, he probably can be saved if he is taken to a veterinarian in time for a series of injections. After the signs appear, however, no cure is possible. The local health

Rats are the carriers of many diseases, including leptospirosis.

department must be notified in the case of a rabid dog, for he is a danger to all who come near him. As with the other shots each year, an annual rabies inoculation is very important. In many areas, the administration of rabies vaccines for dogs is required by law.

PARVOVIRUS

This relatively new virus is a contagious disease that has spread in almost epidemic proportions throughout certain sections of the United States. It has also appeared in Australia, Canada, and Europe. Canine parvovirus attacks the intestinal tract, white blood cells, and heart muscle. It is believed to spread through dog-to-dog contact, and the specific course of infection seems to come from fecal matter of infected dogs. Overcoming parvovirus is difficult, for it is capable of existing in the environment for many months under varying conditions and temperatures, and it can be transmitted from place to place on the hair and feet of infected dogs, as well as on the clothes and shoes of people.

Vomiting and severe diarrhea, which will appear within five to seven days after the animal has been exposed to the virus, are the initial signs of this disease. At the onset of illness, feces will be light gray or yellow-gray in

It is believed that mice can carry the early-stage deer ticks that may be carriers of the dreaded lyme disease.

color, and the urine might be blood-streaked. Because of the vomiting and severe diarrhea, the dog that has contracted the disease will dehydrate quickly. Depression and loss of appetite, as well as a rise in temperature, can accompany the other symptoms. Death caused by this disease usually occurs within 48 to 72 hours following the appearance of the symptoms. Puppies are hardest hit, and the virus is fatal to 75 percent of puppies that contract it. Death in

Stable fly: a painful bite.

puppies can be within two days of the onset of the illness.

A series of shots administered by a veterinarian is the best preventive measure for canine parvovirus. It is also important to disinfect the area where the dog is housed by using one part sodium hypochlorite solution (household bleach) to thirty parts of water and to keep the dog from coming into contact with the fecal matter of other dogs.

Deer tick: a carrier of lyme.

LYME DISEASE

Known as a bacterial infection, Lyme disease is transmitted by ticks infected with a spirochete known as *Borrelia burgdorferi*. The disease is most often acquired by the parasitic bite of an infected deer tick, *Ixodes dammini*. While the range of symptoms is broad, common warning signs include: rash beginning at the bite and soon extending in a bullseye-targetlike fashion; chills, fever, lack of balance, lethargy, and stiffness; swelling and pain, especially in the joints, possibly leading to arthritis or arthritic conditions; heart problems, weak limbs, facial paralysis, and lack of tactile sensation. Although there is no known cure-all, tetracycline and some other drugs have been prescribed with various degrees of success. If you suspect that your dog has Lyme disease, contact your vet immediately.

PARAINFLUENZA

Parainfluenza, or infectious canine tracheobronchitis, is commonly known as "kennel cough." It is highly contagious, affects the upper respiratory system, and is spread through direct or indirect contact with already diseased dogs. It will readily infect dogs of all ages that have not been vaccinated or that were previously infected. While this condition is definitely one of the serious diseases in dogs, it is self-limiting, usually lasting only two to four weeks. The symptoms are high fever and intense, harsh coughing that brings up mucus. As long as your pet sees your veterinarian immediately, the chances for his complete recovery are excellent.

EXTERNAL PARASITES

A parasite is an animal that lives in or on an organism of another species, known as the host, without contributing to the well-being of the host. The majority of dogs' skin problems are parasitic in nature and an estimated 90% of puppies are born with parasites.

Ticks can cause serious problems to dogs where the latter have access to woods, fields, and vegetation in which large numbers of native mammals live. Ticks are usually found clinging to vegetation and attach themselves to animals

Brown dog tick: a common parasite.

Deer fly: a welt-inducing bite.

passing by. They have eight legs and a heavy shield or shell-like covering on their upper surface. Only by keeping dogs away from tick-infested areas can ticks on dogs be prevented.

The flea is the single most common cause of skin and coat problems in dogs. There are 11,000 kinds of fleas which can transmit specific disorders like tapeworm and heartworm or transport smaller parasites onto your dog. The common tapeworm, for example, requires the flea as an intermediate host for completion of its life cycle.

A female flea can lay hundreds of eggs and these will become adults in less than three weeks. Depending on the temperature

The bite of a single flea can cause an irritation that spreads quickly over the surface of the skin. For flea prevention, the dog and his living quarters should be treated regularly.

and the amount of moisture, large numbers of fleas can attack dogs. The ears of dogs, in particular, can play host to hundreds of fleas.

Fleas can lurk in crevices and cracks, carpets, and bedding for months, so frequent cleaning of your dog's environment is absolutely essential. If he is infected by other dogs, then have him bathed and "dipped," which means that he will be put into water containing a chemical that kills fleas. Your veterinarian will advise which dip to use, and your dog must be bathed for at least twenty minutes. These parasites are tenacious and remarkably agile creatures; fleas have existed since prehistoric times and have been found in arctic as well as tropical climates. Some experts claim that fleas can jump 150 times the length of their bodies; this makes them difficult to catch and kill. Thus, treating your pet for parasites without simultaneously

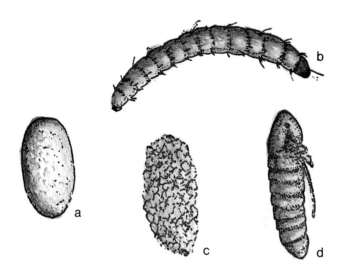

The life cycle of the flea: (a) egg (b) larvae (c) cocoon (d) pupae. If allowed to persist on the dog, fleas will build nests and reproduce, quickly infesting the dog. Regular brushing accompanied by anti-flea applications should suffice to eliminate the flea problem.

treating the environment is both inefficient and ineffective.

INTERNAL PARASITES

Four common internal parasites that may infect a dog are: roundworms, hookworms, whipworms, and tapeworms. The first three can be diagnosed by laboratory examination of the dog's stool, and tapeworms can be seen in the stool or attached to the hair around the anus. When a veterinarian determines what type of worm or worms are present, he then can advise the best treatment.

Roundworms, the dog's most common intestinal parasite, have a life cycle which permits complete eradication by worming twice, ten days apart. The first worming will remove all adults and the second will destroy all subsequently hatched eggs before they, in turn, can produce more parasites.

A dog in good physical condition is less susceptible to worm infestation than a weak dog. Proper sanitation and a nutritious diet help in preventing worms. One of the best preventive measures is to have clean, dry bedding for the dog, as this diminishes the possibility of reinfection due to flea or tick bites.

Health Care

Heartworm infestation in dogs is passed by mosquitoes. Dogs with this disease tire easily, have difficulty in breathing, and lose weight despite a hearty appetite. Administration of preventive medicine throughout the spring, summer, and fall months is advised. A veterinarian must first take a blood sample from the dog to test for the presence of the disease, and if the dog is heartworm-free, pills or liquid medicine can be prescribed.

Heartworm life cycle: a carrier mosquito bites a dog and deposits microfilariae; the filariae travel through the dog's blood stream, lodging in the heart to reproduce. The carrier dog is later bitten by an uninfected mosquito, which thereby acquires uninfectious microfilariae, develops the microfilariae to an infectious stage, bites and infects another dog.

CANINE SENIOR CITIZENS

The processes of aging and gradual degenerative changes start far earlier in a dog than often observed, usually at about seven years of age. If we recall that each year of a dog's life roughly corresponds to about seven years in the life of a man, by the age of seven he is well into middle age. Your pet will become less active, will have a poorer appetite with increased thirst, there will be frequent periods of constipation and less than normal passage of urine. His skin and coat might become dull and dry and his hair will become thin and fall out. There is a tendency towards obesity in old age, which should be avoided by maintaining a regular exercise program. Remember, also, that your pet will be less able to cope

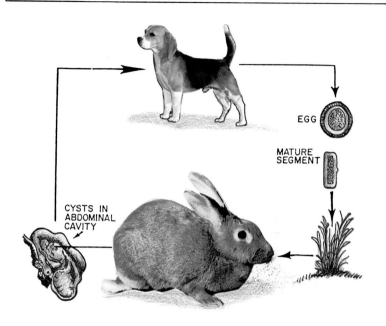

EGG

MATURE SEGMENT

CYSTS IN ABDOMINAL CAVITY

Tapeworms can be acquired in a number of ways; the infected dog must receive veterinary treatment.

with extreme heat, cold, fatigue, and change in routine.

There is the possibility of loss or impairment of hearing or eyesight. He may become bad-tempered more often than in the past. Other ailments such as rheumatism, arthritis, kidney infections, heart disease, male prostatism, and hip dysplasia may occur. Of course, all these require a veterinarian's examination and recommendation of suitable treatment. Care of the teeth is also important in the aging dog.

Indeed, the mouth can be a barometer of nutritional health. Degenerating gums, heavy tartar on the teeth, loose teeth, and sore lips are common. The worst of all diseases in old age, however, is neglect. Good care in early life will have its effect on your dog's later years; the nutrition and general health care of his first few years can determine his lifespan and the quality of his life. It is worth bearing in mind that the older, compared to the younger, animal needs more protein of good biological value, more vitamins A, B-complex, D and E, more calcium and iron, less fat and fewer carbohydrates.

Preventive Dental Care

 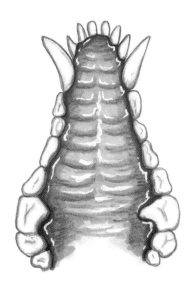

ALL DOGS NEED TO CHEW

Puppies and young dogs need something with resistance to chew on while their teeth and jaws are developing—to cut the puppy teeth, to induce growth of the permanent teeth under the puppy teeth, to assist in getting rid of the puppy teeth on time, to help the permanent teeth through the gums, to assure normal jaw development and to settle the permanent teeth solidly in the jaws.

The adult dog's desire to chew stems from the instinct for tooth cleaning, gum massage, and jaw exercise—plus the need to vent periodic doggie tensions. . . . A pacifier if you will!

Dental caries, as they affect the teeth of humans, are virtually

It is imperative that the owner take the necessary measures to ensure sound dental health. Ideal canine dentition illustrated: upper palate on right; lower palate on left.

unknown in dogs; but tartar (calculus) accumulates on the teeth of dogs, particularly at the gum line, more rapidly than on the teeth of humans. These accumulations, if not removed, bring irritation and then infection, which erode the tooth enamel and ultimately destroy the teeth at the roots. It is important that you take your dog to your local veterinarian for periodic dental examinations.

Tooth and jaw development will normally continue until the dog is more than a year old—but sometimes much longer, depending upon the dog, its chewing exercise, rate of calcium utilization and many other factors, known and unknown, which affect the development of individual dogs. Diseases, like distemper for example, may sometimes arrest development of the teeth and jaws, which may resume months or even years later.

This is why dogs, especially puppies and young dogs, will often destroy valuable property when their chewing instinct is not diverted from their owners'

his instinct tells him to chew. If your purposes, and those of your dog, are to be accomplished, what you provide for chewing must be desirable from the doggie viewpoint, have the necessary functional qualities, and, above all, be safe.

It is very important that dogs be prohibited from chewing on anything they can break or indigestible things from which they can bite sizeable chunks. Sharp pieces, such as those from a bone which can be broken by a dog, may pierce the intestinal wall and kill.

possessions, particularly during the widely varying critical period for young dogs. Saving your possessions from destruction, assuring proper development of teeth and jaws, providing for "interim" tooth cleaning and gum massage, and channeling doggie tensions into a non-destructive outlet are, therefore, all dependent upon the dog's having something suitable for chewing readily available when

A dog's teeth with little to no calculus build-up, a state achievable through consistent and appropriate care.

Indigestible things which can be bitten off in chunks, such as toys made of rubber compound or cheap plastic, may cause an intestinal stoppage; if not regurgitated, they are certain to bring painful death unless surgery is promptly performed.

NATURAL CHEW BONES

Strong natural bones, such as 4- to 8-inch lengths of round shin bone from mature beef—either the kind you can get from your butcher or one of the varieties available commercially in pet stores—may serve your dog's teething needs, if his mouth is large enough to handle them.

You may be tempted to give your puppy a smaller bone and he may not be able to break it when you do, but puppies grow rapidly and the power of their jaws constantly increases until maturity. This means that a growing dog may break one of the smaller bones at any time, swallow the pieces and die painfully before you realize what is wrong.

Many people have the mistaken notion that their dog's teeth are like those of wild carnivores or of dogs from antiquity. The teeth of wild carnivorous animals and those found in the fossils of the dog-like creatures of antiquity have far thicker and stronger enamel than those of our dogs today.

All hard natural bones are highly abrasive. If your dog is an avid chewer, natural bones may wear away his teeth prematurely; hence, they then should be taken away from your dog when the teething purposes have been served. The badly worn, and usually painful, teeth of many mature dogs can be traced to excessive chewing on animal bones. Contrary to popular belief, knuckle bones that can be chewed up and swallowed by the dog provide little, if any, useable calcium or other nutrient. They do, however, disturb the digestion of most dogs and might cause them to vomit the nourishing food they really need.

Never give a dog your old shoe to chew on, even if you have removed all the nails or metal parts, such as lace grommets, buckles, metal arches, and so on. Rubber heels are especially dangerous, as the dog can bite off chunks, swallow them, and suffer from intestinal blockage as a result. Additionally, if the rubber should happen to have a nail imbedded in it that you cannot detect, this could pierce or tear the intestinal wall. There is always the possibility, too, that your dog may fail to differentiate between his shoe and yours and chew up a good pair while you're not looking. It is strongly recommended that you refrain from offering old shoes as chew toys, since there are much safer products available.

RAWHIDE CHEWS

The most popular material from which dog chews are made is the hide from cows, horses, and other animals. Most of these chews are made in foreign countries where the quality of the hide is not good enough for

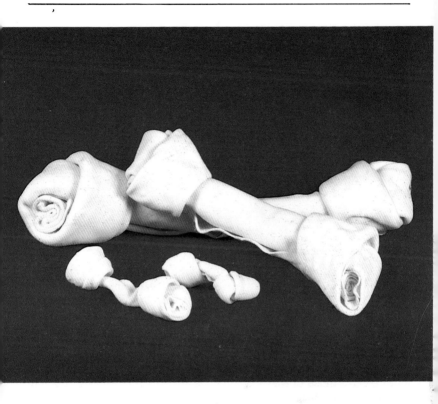

Many dogs love rawhide, and many stores carry a variety of rawhide chew products.

making leather. These foreign hides may contain lead, antibiotics, arsenic, or insecticides which might be detrimental to the health of your dog . . . or even your children. It is not impossible that a small child will start chewing on a piece of rawhide meant for the dog! Rawhide chews do not serve the primary chewing functions very well. They are also a bit messy when wet from mouthing, and most dogs chew them up rather rapidly. They have been considered safe for dogs until recently.

Rawhide is flavorful to dogs. They like it. Currently, some veterinarians have been attributing cases of acute constipation to large pieces of incompletely digested rawhide in ·the intestine. Basically it is good for them to chew on, but dogs think rawhide is food. They do not play with it nor do they use it as a pacifier to relieve doggie tension. They eat it as they would any other food. This is dangerous, for the hide is very difficult for dogs to digest and swallow, and many dogs choke on large particles of rawhide that become stuck in their throats. *Before you offer your dog rawhide chews, consult your veterinarian.* Vets have a lot of

Annealed nylon chews are recommended by veterinarians as proven-safe and effective canine chew devices.

experience with canine chewing devices; ask them what they recommend.

NYLON CHEW DEVICES

The nylon bones, especially those with natural meat and bone flavor added, are probably the most complete, safe, and economical answer to the

chewing need. Dogs cannot break them nor bite off sizeable chunks; hence, they are completely safe. And being longer lasting than other things offered for the purpose, they are very economical.

Hard chewing raises little bristle-like projections on the surface of the nylon bones to provide effective interim tooth cleaning and vigorous gum massage, much in the same way your toothbrush does it for you. The little projections are raked off and swallowed in the form of thin shavings, but the chemistry of the nylon is such that they break down in the stomach fluids and pass through without effect.

The toughness of the nylon provides the strong chewing resistance needed for important jaw exercise and effective help for the teething functions; however, there is no tooth wear because nylon is non-abrasive. Being inert, nylon does not support the growth of microorganisms, and it can be washed in soap and water or sterilized by boiling or in an autoclave.

There are a great variety of Nylabone® products available that veterinarians recommend as safe and healthy for your dog or puppy to chew on. These Nylabone® Pooch Pacifiers® usually don't splinter, chip, or break off in large chunks; instead, they are frizzled by the

One of the many advantages of annealed nylon chew products is durability and long life. To keep your Nylabone® products sterile and to re-energize their flavor, these bones can be boiled in broth.

dog's chewing action, and this creates a toothbrush-like surface that cleanses the teeth and massages the gums. At the same time, these hard-nylon therapeutic devices channel doggie tension and chewing frustation into constructive rather than destructive behavior. The original nylon bone (Nylabone®) is not a toy and dogs use it only when in need of pacification. Keeping a bone in each of your dog's recreation rooms is the best method of providing the requisite pacification. Unfortunately, many nylon chew products have been copied. These inferior quality copies are sold in supermarkets and other chain stores. The really good products are sold only through veterinarians, pet shops, grooming salons and places where the sales people really know something about dogs. The good products have the flavor impregnated *into* the bone. This makes the taste last longer. The smell is undetectable

to humans. The artificial bones
which have a strong odor are
poor-quality bones with the odor
sprayed on to impress the dog
owner (not the dog)! These
heavily scented dog toys may
impart the odor to your carpets
or furniture if an odor-sprayed
bone lies there wet from a dog's
chewing on it.

*Food particles can be deposited between the teeth, where they
are difficult to remove. Even the best chew products may not be
able to free these decaying food pieces. For this reason, the Ny-
lafloss® dental device is recommended. It is the only effective
product to clean between the dog's teeth.*

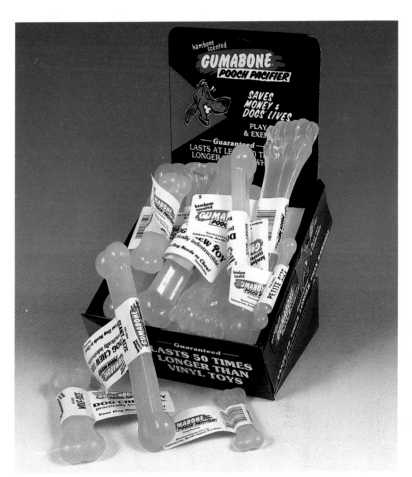

*While satisfying the deep-rooted desire to chew, the dog's chewing a Gumabone®
works to prevent tartar and plaque build-up. A dog should have access to an effective chew product at all times.*

FLOSS OR LOSS!

Most dentists relay that
brushing daily is just not enough.
In order to prevent unnecessary
tooth loss, flossing is essential.
For dogs, human dental floss is
not the answer—however,

canine dental devices are
available. The Nylafloss® is a
revolutionary product that is
designed to save dogs teeth and
keep them healthy. Even though
your dogs won't believe you,
Nylafloss® is not a toy but rather

145

Preventive Dental Care

Prevention is the key to good dental health. It makes little sense to ignore your dog's dental needs; tooth problems can be costly and detrimental to your dog's well being. Nylafloss® is one very important part of preventive dental care.

a most effective agent in removing destructive plaque between the teeth and *beneath* the gum line where gum disease begins. Gentle tugging is all that is necessary to activate the Nylafloss®. These 100% inert nylon products are guaranteed to outlast rawhide chews by ten times and are available for sale at all pet shops.

THE IMPORTANCE OF PREVENTION

In order to get to the root of canine dentistry problems, it is important for owners to realize that no less than 75% of all canine dental health problems serious enough to require a vet's assistance and nearly 98% of all canine teeth lost are attributable to periodontal disease. Periodontal disease not only mars the teeth but also the gums and other buccal tissue in the mouth. Severe cases of periodontal disease involve resultant bacterial toxins which are absorbed into the blood stream and cause permanent damage to the heart and kidneys. In the infected mouth, teeth are loosened; tartar, unsightly and bad smelling, accumulates heavily; and the dog experiences a complete loss of appetite. Long-standing periodontitis can also manifest itself in simple symptoms such as diarrhea and vomiting.

Periodontal disease deserves the attention of every dog owner—a dog's teeth are extremely important to his ongoing health. The accumulation of plaque, food matter mixed with saliva attaching itself to the tooth surface, is a sure sign of potential bacteria build-up. As toxic material gathers, the bone surrounding the teeth erodes. If plaque and calculus continue to reside without attention, bacteria-fighting cells will form residual pus at the root of the teeth, dividing the gum from the tooth. The debris is toxic and actually kills the buccal tissue. This is a most undesirable situation, as hardened dental calculus is one of the most direct causative agents of periodontitis.

In actuality, the disease is a result of a number of contributing factors. Old age, a diet comprised solely of soft or semi-soft foods, dental tartar, constant chewing of hair and even coprophagy (the eating of stool) are among the most common contributors.

Just as regular dental visits and brushing are necessary for humans, regular hygienic care and veterinary check-ups can help control tooth problems in canines. Involved and expensive routines can be performed on the affected, neglected mouth and teeth if decay has begun eroding the enamel and infecting the gums. Cleaning, polishing, and scaling are routine to remove calculus build-up.

Owners must claim responsibility for their dog's health, and tooth care is no small aspect of the care required. Daily brushing with a salt/baking soda solution is the best answer, but many owners find this tedious or just too difficult to perform. The simpler and more proven effective way to avoid, reduce, and fight periodontal disease and calculus build-up is giving the dog regular access to a thermoplastic polymer chew device. The Gumabone® products are the only scientifically proven line that offers the desired protection from calculus and tartar build-up.

CANINE DENTAL BREAKTHROUGH

The independent research of Dr. Andrew Duke, D.V.M., reveals that 70% of the dogs that regularly use Gumabone® experience a reduction of calculus build-up. This find is a breakthrough for the dog world, since the Gumabone® has already resided in the toy boxes of many dogs as their favorite play item. Little did owners know previously that their dogs were gaining entertainment and unparalleled dental treatment at the same time. Dr. Duke writes: "There is little debate left that

THE CALCULUS INDEX

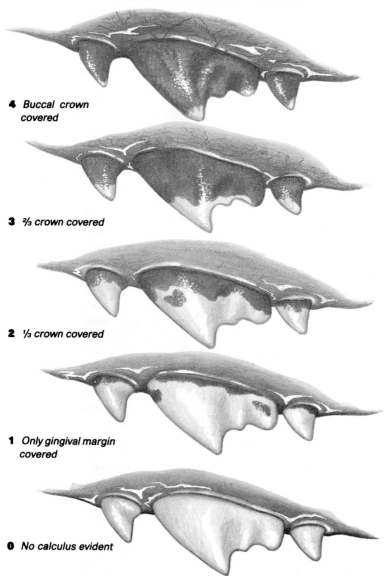

4 *Buccal crown covered*

3 *⅔ crown covered*

2 *⅓ crown covered*

1 *Only gingival margin covered*

0 *No calculus evident*

*An artist's representation of the calculus index, ranging from index rating **4** (topmost drawing) through index rating **0** (lowest drawing).*

dental calculus is an excellent indicator of periodontal health in the dog, just as it is in humans. "Calculus does not cause gingivitis and periodontitis, but the plaque and bacteria that cause periodontitis are responsible for the mineral precipitation we know as 'calculus.' All veterinarians who have made a study of dogs' oral

A dog's teeth showing a moderate calculus build-up.

health have noticed the middle aged dog who actively chews with excellent gingival health. Many of these dogs that chew hard substances regularly wear the cusps down and even may expose the pulp cavity faster than secondary dentin can be formed. Often these 'excellent chewers' are presented with slab fractures of the premolars or apical abcesses.

"The challenge then becomes to find a substance which is effective in removing calculus and plaque but does not wear the enamel excessively. In an attempt to duplicate the chewstuffs enjoyed by dogs in the wild, researchers have used bovine tracheas to demonstrate the inhibition of plaque and gingivitis. Very little else has been done in veterinary medicine to establish a scientific basis for evaluating chewstuffs.

"In the human field it is generally accepted (incorrectly) that fibrous foodstuffs and diet have no effect on oral health. This is a moot point since the practice of brushing is by far a more efficient technique of preventing plaque accumulation, calculus and periodontal disease. Studies in human subjects failed to find any benefits in eating apples, raw carrots, etc. If people are not allowed to brush, it is difficult to conduct clinical trials of more than one week.

"The increased awareness of animals' dental health of recent years has resulted in most veterinary practitioners' recommending some kind of chewstuff to their dog owners. To meet this market demand, there has been a stampede into the market by vendors ready to promote their products. The veterinarian is furnished no

Plaque is formed by the food debris and bacterial deposits on the teeth. Due to the high carbon dioxide and pH level in the mouth, minerals precipitate on the plaque to form calculus.

scientific data, but is asked to promote rawhide, bounce, and squeaky toys. How would our human colleagues handle this situation? Can Listerine® say that it prevents colds, but not support the claim? Can Tartar Control Crest® or Colgate Tartar Control Formula® be sold if it is not proven that it does in fact reduce tartar? Of course not.

"To this end, the following study was made.

"*Method:* Twenty dogs of different breeds and age were selected from a veterinary practice's clientele. Although most were from multiple pet households, none were colony dogs. The owners were asked if they would allow their dogs to be anesthetized for two prophylactic cleanings which included root planing, polishing, and gingival debridement necessary to insure good oral hygiene.

"The dogs were divided into two groups of 10. Their teeth were cleaned and their calculus index converted to 0. One group was allowed only their normal dry commercial dog ration for 30 days. The other was allowed to have free choice access to Gumabone® products of the appropriate size.

"After 30 days, photoslides were made of the upper 3rd premolar, upper 4th premolar, and the lower 4th premolar on both sides of the dog's mouth. The dogs were again subjected to a prophylactic cleaning and the group reversed. After the second 30 days, photoslides were again made. A total of six teeth in each mouth were evaluated on each dog. This was 80 slides representing 240 teeth."

Fourteen out of 20 dogs (or 70%) experienced a reduction in calculus build-up by regularly

Teeth of affected canine showing little to no plaque or calculus build-up after professional cleaning.

Regular use of the Gumabone® chew products can significantly reduce plaque build-up.

using the Gumabone® product. These products are available in a variety of sizes (for different size dogs) and designed in interesting shapes: bones, balls, knots and rings (and even a tug toy). The entertainment value of the Gumabone® products is but an added advantage to the fighting of tooth decay and periodontitis. The products are ham-flavored and made of a thermoplastic polymer that is designed to outlast by ten times any other rawhide, rubber or vinyl chew product, none of which can promise the proven benefit of the Gumabone®.

If your dog is able to chew apart a Gumabone®, it is probable that you provided him with a bone that is too small for him. Replace it with a larger one and the problem should not re-

Above: The clean healthy teeth that are desired in dogs should inspire owners to work towards better dental hygiene. *Below:* The beginning of undesirable deposits forming on improperly maintained teeth.

materialize. Economically, the Gumabone® is a smart choice, even without comparing it to the cost of extensive dental care.

Of course, nothing can *substitute* for periodic professional attention to your dog's teeth and gums, no more than your toothbrush can replace your dentist. Have your dog's teeth cleaned by your veterinarian at least once a year—twice a year is better—and he will be healthier, happier, and a far more pleasant companion.

Gumabones® are available through veterinarians and pet shops.

Breeding

If you own a bitch and you want to breed her, first make sure you can handle the responsibility of caring for her and her litter of pups. Consider the time and money involved just to get her into breeding condition and then to sustain her throughout pregnancy and afterwards while she tends her young. You will be obligated to house, feed, groom, and housebreak the puppies until good homes can be found for them; and, lest we forget, there will be periodic trips to the vet for check-ups, wormings, and inoculations. Common sense should tell you that it is indeed cruel to bring unwanted or unplanned puppies into an already crowded canine world; only negligent pet owners allow this to happen. With pet-quality purebred dogs, most breeders require prospective pet owners to sign a neuter/spay agreement when they purchase their dogs. In this way breeders can be assured that only their very best stock of show-quality and breeder-quality animals, i.e., those that match closely their individual standards of perfection and those that are free of genetic disorders or disease, will be used to propagate the breed.

Before you select a stud to mate with your bitch, think carefully about why you want her to give birth to a litter of puppies. If you feel she will be deprived in some way if she is not bred, if you think your children will learn from the experience, if you have the mistaken notion that you will make money from this great undertaking, think again. A dog can lead a perfectly happy, healthy, normal life without having been mated; in fact, spaying a female and neutering a male helps them become better pets, as they are not so anxious to search for a mate in an effort to relieve their sexual tensions. As for giving the children a lesson in sex education, this is hardly a valid reason for breeding your dog. And on an economic level, it takes not only years of hard work (researching pedigrees and bloodlines, studying genetics, among other things), but it takes plenty of capital (money, equipment, facilities) to make a decent profit from dog breeding. Why most dedicated breeders are lucky just to break even. If you have only a casual interest in dog breeding, it is best to leave this pastime to those who are more experienced in such matters, those who consider it a serious hobby or vocation. If you have bought a breeder– or show-quality canine, one that may be capable of producing champions, and if you are just starting out with this breeding venture, seek advice from the seller of your dog, from other veteran breeders, and from your vet before you begin.

Breeding

THE FEMALE "IN SEASON"

A bitch may come into season (also known as "heat" or estrus) once or several times a year, depending on the particular breed and the individual dog. Her first seasonal period, that is to say, the time when she is capable of being fertilized by a male dog, may occur as early as six months with some breeds. If you own a female and your

portion of the female's reproductive tract; the soft, flabby vulva indicates her readiness to mate. Around this second week or so ovulation occurs, and this is the crucial period for her to be bred, if this is what you have in mind for her. It is during this middle phase of the heat cycle when conception can take place. Just remember that there is great variation from

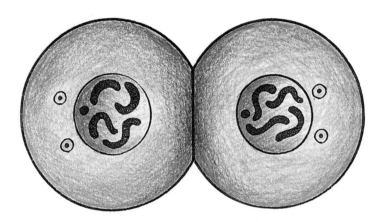

intention is *not* to breed her, by all means discuss with the vet the possibility of having her spayed: this means before she reaches sexual maturity.

The first sign of the female's being in season is a thin red discharge, which may increase for about a week; it then changes color to a thin yellowish stain, which lasts about another week. Simultaneously, there is a swelling of the vulva, the exterior

Cells reproduce by a process called mitosis, in which the cells divide, forming two identical cells.

bitch to bitch with regard to how often they come into heat, how long the heat cycles last, how long the period of ovulation lasts, and how much time elapses between heat cycles. Generally, after the third week of heat, the vulval swelling decreases and the estrus period

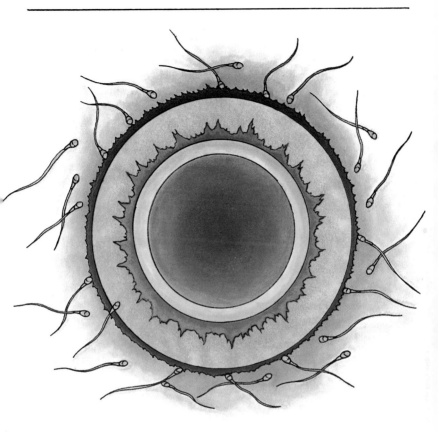

ceases for several months.

It should be mentioned that the female will probably lose her puppy coat, or at least shed part of it, about three months after she has come into season. This is the time when her puppies would have been weaned, had she been mated, and females generally drop coat at this time.

With female dogs, there are few, if any, behavioral changes during estrus. A bitch may dart out of an open door to greet all

The egg within the female is surrounded by a wall that normally takes many sperm to penetrate. In this way, only the strongest sperm will fertilize the egg. A fertile female in season usually has a number of eggs, known as gametes.

available male dogs that show an interest in her, and she may occasionally raise her tail and assume a mating stance, particularly if you pet her lower back; but these signs are not as dramatic as those of the sexually mature male. He himself does not experience heat cycles; rather, he is attracted to the female during all phases of her seasonal period. He usually becomes more aggressive and tends to fight with other males, especially over females in heat. He tends to mark his territory with urine to attract females and at the same time to warn other competitive males. It is not uncommon to see him mount various objects, and people, in an effort to satisfy his mature sexual urges.

If you are a homeowner and you have an absolutely climb-proof and dig-proof run within your yard, it may be safe to leave your bitch in season there. But then again it may not be a wise idea, as there have been cases of males mating with females right through chain-link fencing! Just to be on the safe side, shut her indoors during her heat periods and don't let her outdoors until you are certain the estrus period is over. Never leave a bitch in heat outdoors, unsupervised, even for a minute so that she can defecate or

A whelping box provides the female with a safe place to deliver her pups. Introduce the female to the box several days prior to delivery to get her adjusted to it. Later, when whelping is near, move her to the box so that she may prepare for delivery.

While in the womb, each pup is encased within a protective sac.

urinate. If you want to prevent the neighborhood dogs from hanging around your doorstep, as they inevitably will do when they discover your female is in season, take her some distance away from the house before you let her do her business. Otherwise, these canine suitors will be attracted to her by the arousing odor of her urine, and they will know instinctively that she isn't far from her scented "calling card." If you need to walk your bitch, take her in the car to a nearby park or field for a chance to stretch her legs. Remember that after about three weeks, and this varies from dog to dog, you can let her outdoors again with no worry that she can have puppies until the next heat period.

Breeding

WHEN TO BREED

It is usually best to breed a bitch when she comes into her second or third season. Plan in advance the time of year which is best for you, taking into account your own schedule of activities (vacations, business trips, social engagements, and so on). Make sure you will be able to set aside plenty of time to assist with whelping of the newborn pups and caring for the dam and her litter for the next few weeks. At the very least, it probably will take an hour or so each day just to feed and clean up after the brood—but undoubtedly you will find it takes much longer if you stop to admire and play with the youngsters periodically! Refrain from selling the litter until it is at least six weeks old, keeping in mind that a litter of pups takes up a fair amount of space by then. It will be your responsibility to provide for them until they have been weaned from their mother, properly socialized, housebroken, and ready to go to new homes (unless you plan to keep them all). Hopefully, as strongly recommended, you will have already lined up buyers for the pups in advance of their arrival into this world.

CHOOSING THE STUD

You can plan to breed your female about six-and-one-half months after the start of her last season, although a variation of a month or two either way is not unusual. Do some research into the various bloodlines within your breed and then choose a stud dog and make arrangements well in advance. If you are breeding for show stock, which will command higher prices than pet-quality animals, a mate should be chosen very carefully. He should complement any deficiencies (bad traits) that your female may have, and he should have a good show record or be the sire of show winners, if he is old enough to have proven himself. If possible, the bitch and stud should have several ancestors in common within the last two or three generations, as such combinations have been known, generally, to "click" best.

The owner of a stud dog usually charges a stud fee for use of the animal's services. This does not always guarantee a litter, but if she fails to conceive, chances are you may be able to breed your female to that stud

Facing page: Dogs have an average gestation period of 63 to 65 days. This chart gives the expected delivery date according to the date on which the bitch was mated. The due date is an approximation only, and the owner should be prepared well in advance of the due date, especially with first-time mothers. If a bitch is mated more than once, the owner should use the date of the first mating but realize the possibility of a later delivery.

PERPETUAL WHELPING CHART

	1	2	3	4	5	6	7	8	9	10	11	12	13	14	15	16	17	18	19	20	21	22	23	24	25	26	27	28	29	30	31
Bred—Jan.	1	2	3	4	5	6	7	8	9	10	11	12	13	14	15	16	17	18	19	20	21	22	23	24	25	26	27	28	29	30	31
Due—March	5	6	7	8	9	10	11	12	13	14	15	16	17	18	19	20	21	22	23	24	25	26	27	28	29	30	31	Apr 1	Apr 2	Apr 3	Apr 4
Bred—Feb.	1	2	3	4	5	6	7	8	9	10	11	12	13	14	15	16	17	18	19	20	21	22	23	24	25	26	27	28			
Due—April	5	6	7	8	9	10	11	12	13	14	15	16	17	18	19	20	21	22	23	24	25	26	27	28	29	30	May 1	May 2			
Bred—Mar.	1	2	3	4	5	6	7	8	9	10	11	12	13	14	15	16	17	18	19	20	21	22	23	24	25	26	27	28	29	30	31
Due—May	3	4	5	6	7	8	9	10	11	12	13	14	15	16	17	18	19	20	21	22	23	24	25	26	27	28	29	30	31	Jun 1	Jun 2
Bred—Apr.	1	2	3	4	5	6	7	8	9	10	11	12	13	14	15	16	17	18	19	20	21	22	23	24	25	26	27	28	29	30	
Due—June	3	4	5	6	7	8	9	10	11	12	13	14	15	16	17	18	19	20	21	22	23	24	25	26	27	28	29	30	Jul 1	Jul 2	
Bred—May	1	2	3	4	5	6	7	8	9	10	11	12	13	14	15	16	17	18	19	20	21	22	23	24	25	26	27	28	29	30	31
Due—July	3	4	5	6	7	8	9	10	11	12	13	14	15	16	17	18	19	20	21	22	23	24	25	26	27	28	29	30	31	Aug 1	Aug 2
Bred—June	1	2	3	4	5	6	7	8	9	10	11	12	13	14	15	16	17	18	19	20	21	22	23	24	25	26	27	28	29	30	
Due—August	3	4	5	6	7	8	9	10	11	12	13	14	15	16	17	18	19	20	21	22	23	24	25	26	27	28	29	30	31	Sep 1	
Bred—July	1	2	3	4	5	6	7	8	9	10	11	12	13	14	15	16	17	18	19	20	21	22	23	24	25	26	27	28	29	30	31
Due—September	2	3	4	5	6	7	8	9	10	11	12	13	14	15	16	17	18	19	20	21	22	23	24	25	26	27	28	29	30	Oct 1	Oct 2
Bred—Aug.	1	2	3	4	5	6	7	8	9	10	11	12	13	14	15	16	17	18	19	20	21	22	23	24	25	26	27	28	29	30	31
Due—October	3	4	5	6	7	8	9	10	11	12	13	14	15	16	17	18	19	20	21	22	23	24	25	26	27	28	29	30	31	Nov 1	Nov 2
Bred—Sept.	1	2	3	4	5	6	7	8	9	10	11	12	13	14	15	16	17	18	19	20	21	22	23	24	25	26	27	28	29	30	
Due—November	3	4	5	6	7	8	9	10	11	12	13	14	15	16	17	18	19	20	21	22	23	24	25	26	27	28	29	30	Dec 1	Dec 2	
Bred—Oct.	1	2	3	4	5	6	7	8	9	10	11	12	13	14	15	16	17	18	19	20	21	22	23	24	25	26	27	28	29	30	31
Due—December	3	4	5	6	7	8	9	10	11	12	13	14	15	16	17	18	19	20	21	22	23	24	25	26	27	28	29	30	31	Jan 1	Jan 2
Bred—Nov.	1	2	3	4	5	6	7	8	9	10	11	12	13	14	15	16	17	18	19	20	21	22	23	24	25	26	27	28	29	30	
Due—January	3	4	5	6	7	8	9	10	11	12	13	14	15	16	17	18	19	20	21	22	23	24	25	26	27	28	29	30	31	Feb 1	
Bred—Dec.	1	2	3	4	5	6	7	8	9	10	11	12	13	14	15	16	17	18	19	20	21	22	23	24	25	26	27	28	29	30	31
Due—February	2	3	4	5	6	7	8	9	10	11	12	13	14	15	16	17	18	19	20	21	22	23	24	25	26	27	28	Mar 1	Mar 2	Mar 3	Mar 4

again. In some instances the owner of the stud will agree to take a "first pick of the litter" in place of a fee. You should, of course, settle all details beforehand, including the possibility of a single puppy surviving, deciding the age at which the pup is to be taken, and so forth.

If you plan to raise a litter that will be sold exclusively as pets,

and if you merely plan to make use of an available male (not a top stud dog), the most important selection point involves temperament. Make sure the dog is friendly, as well as healthy, because a bad disposition can be passed on to his puppies—and this is the worst of all traits in a dog destined to be a pet. If you are breeding pet-quality dogs, a "stud fee puppy," not necessarily the choice of the litter, is the usual payment. Don't

The reproductive system of the female dog consists of a highly specialized group of organs situated at the rear of the animal.

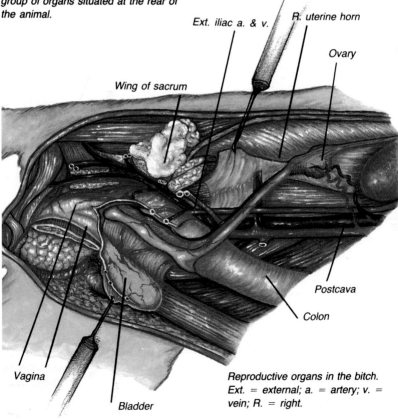

Reproductive organs in the bitch. Ext. = external; a. = artery; v. = vein; R. = right.

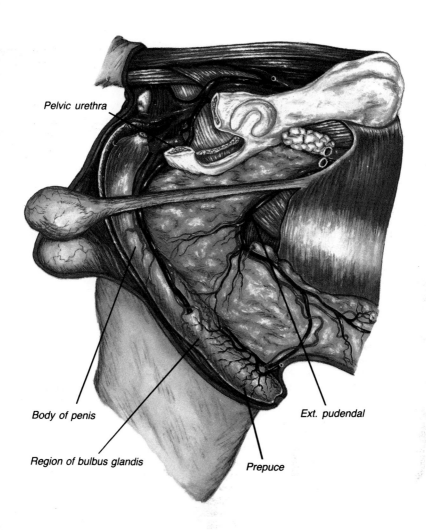

Pelvic urethra

Body of penis

Region of bulbus glandis

Ext. pudendal

Prepuce

The reproductive system of the male dog includes the penis and testicles. The sperm and testosterone producing testes are contained within the scrotal sac. When not excited, the penis is withdrawn into the dog. The dog's penis is unique in that the base of the shaft has a bulbous swelling that forbids retraction from the vagina until some time has passed after intercourse.

breed indiscriminately; be sure you will be able to find good homes for each of the pups, or be sure you have the facilities to keep them yourself, *before* you plan to mate your dog.

PREPARATION FOR BREEDING

Before you breed your female, make sure she is in good health.

She should be neither too thin nor too fat. Any skin disease *must* be cured first so that it is not passed on to the puppies. If she has worms, she should be wormed before being bred or within three weeks after the mating. It is generally considered a good idea to revaccinate her against distemper and hepatitis before the puppies are born. This will increase the immunity the puppies receive during their early, most vulnerable period.

The female will probably be ready to breed twelve days after the first colored discharge appears. You can usually make arrangements to board her with the owner of the stud for a few days, to insure her being there at the proper time; or you can take her to be mated and bring her home the same day if you live near enough to the stud's owner. If the bitch still appears receptive she may be bred again two days later, just to make certain the mating was successful. However, some females never show signs of willingness, so it helps to have an experienced breeder on hand. In fact, you both may have to assist with the

The canine uterus is quite different from the human uterus. Besides the difference in shape, the canine uterus is designed to house an average of five to eight offspring.

OVARY

HORN OF UTERUS

BLADDER —

BODY OF UTERUS

CANINE UTERUS
Before mating

VAGINA

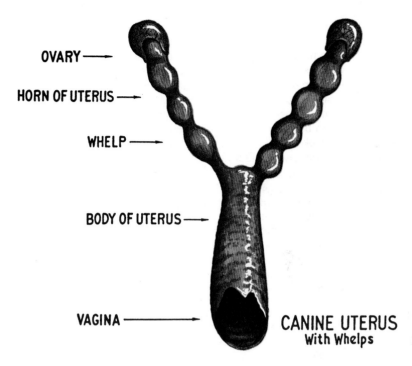

OVARY →

HORN OF UTERUS →

WHELP →

BODY OF UTERUS →

VAGINA → **CANINE UTERUS**
With Whelps

Prior to birth, the developing pups are housed in the horns of the uterus.

mating by holding the animals against each other to ensure the "tie" is not broken, that is, to make certain copulation takes place. Sometimes, too, you'll need to muzzle the bitch to keep her from biting you or the stud.

Usually the second day after the discharge changes color is the proper time to mate the bitch, and she may be bred for about three days following this time. For an additional week or so, she may have some discharge and attract other dogs by her odor; but she should not be bred. Once she has been bred, keep her far from all other male dogs, as they have the capacity to impregnate her again and sire some of her puppies. This could prove disastrous where purebred puppies— especially show-quality ones— are concerned.

THE FEMALE IN WHELP

You can expect the puppies nine weeks from the day of the mating, although sixty-one days is as common as sixty-three. Gestation, that period when the pups are developing inside their mother, varies among individual bitches. During this time the female should receive normal care and exercise. If she was overweight at the start, don't increase her food right away; excess weight at whelping time can be a problem with some dogs. If she is on the thin side, however, supplement her meal or meals with a portion of milk and biscuit at noontime. This will help build her up and put weight on her.

You may want to add a mineral and vitamin supplement to her diet, on the advice of your veterinarian, since she will need an extra supply not only for herself but for the puppies growing inside of her. As the mother's appetite increases, feed her more. During the last two weeks of pregnancy, the pups grow enormously and the mother will have little room for food and less of an appetite. She should be tempted with meat, liver, and milk, however.

As the female in whelp grows heavier, cut out violent exercise

Using simple genetic rules, an owner can predict to some degree the traits that the offspring of a given mating can exhibit. The six possible ways in which a pair of determiners can unite are illustrated on this Mendelian expectation chart. Ratios apply to expectancy over large numbers, except in lines 1, 2, and 6 where exact expectancy is realized in every litter.

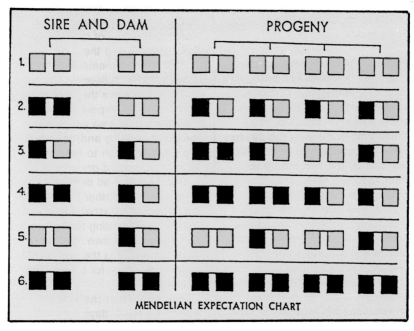

MENDELIAN EXPECTATION CHART

and jumping from her usual routine. Although a dog used to such activities will often play with the children or run around voluntarily, restrain her for her own sake.

A sign that whelping is imminent is the loss of hair around her breasts. This is nature's way of "clearing a path" so that the puppies will be able to find their source of nourishment. As parturition draws near, the breasts will have swelled with milk and the nipples will have enlarged and darkened to a rosy pink. If the hair in the breast region does not shed for some reason, you can easily cut it short with a pair of scissors or comb it out so that it does not mat and become a hindrance to the suckling pups later on.

PREPARING FOR THE PUPPIES

Prepare a whelping box a few days before the puppies are due, and allow the mother to sleep there overnight or to spend some time in it during the day to become accustomed to it. This way she is less likely to try to have her pups under the front porch or in the middle of your bed. A variety of places will serve, such as the corner of your cellar or garage (provided these places are warm and dry). An unused room, such as a dimly lit spare bedroom, can also serve as the place for delivery. If the weather is warm, a large outdoor dog house will do, as long as it is well protected from rain, drafts, and the cold—and enclosed by fencing or a run. A whelping box serves to separate mother and puppies from visitors and other distractions. The walls should be high enough to restrain the puppies yet low enough to allow the mother to take a short respite from her brood after she has fed them. Four feet square is minimum size (for most dogs) and six-to-eight-inch high walls will keep the pups in until they begin to climb; then side walls should be built up so that the young ones cannot wander away from their nest. As the puppies grow, they really need more room anyway, so double the space with a very low partition down the middle of the box, and soon you will find them naturally housebreaking themselves. Puppies rarely relieve themselves where they sleep. Layers of newspapers spread over the whole area will make excellent bedding and be absorbent enough to keep the surface warm and dry. These should be removed daily and replaced with another thick layer. An old quilt or washable blanket makes better footing for the nursing puppies than slippery newspaper during the first week; this is also softer for the mother to lie on.

Be prepared for the actual whelping several days in

advance. Usually the mother will tear up papers, refuse food, and become restless. These may be false alarms; the real test is her temperature, which will drop to below 100°F (38°C) about twelve hours before whelping. Take her temperature with a rectal thermometer, morning and evening, and usher her to her whelping box when her temperature goes down. Keep a close watch on her and make sure she stays safely indoors (or outdoors in a safe enclosure); if she is let outside, unleashed, or allowed to roam freely, she could wander off and start to go into labor. It is possible that she could whelp anywhere, and this could be unfortunate if she needs your assistance.

WHELPING

Usually little help is needed from you, but it is wise to stay close to be sure that the mother's lack of experience (if this is her first time) does not cause an unnecessary complication. Be ready to help when the first puppy arrives, for it could smother if she does not break the amniotic membrane enclosing it. She should tear open the sac and start licking the puppy, drying and stimulating it. Check to see that all fluids have been cleared from the pup's nostrils and mouth after the mother has licked her youngster clean; otherwise the pup may

have difficulty breathing. If the mother fails to tear open the sac and stimulate the newborn's breathing, you can do this yourself by tearing the sack with your hands and then gently rubbing the infant with a soft, rough towel. The afterbirth attached to the puppy by the long umbilical cord should follow the birth of each puppy. Watch to be sure that each afterbirth is expelled, for the retention of this material can cause infection. In her instinct for cleanliness the mother will probably eat the afterbirth after severing the umbilical cord. One or two meals of this will not hurt her; they stimulate her milk supply, as well as labor, for remaining pups. However, eating too many afterbirths can make her lose appetite for the food she needs to feed her pups and regain her strength. So remove the rest of them, along with the wet newspapers, and keep the box dry and clean.

If the mother does not bite the cord or bites it too close to the puppy's body, take over the job to prevent an umbilical hernia. Tearing is recommended, but you can cut the cord, about two inches from the body, with a sawing motion with scissors that have been sterilized in alcohol. Then dip the end of the cut cord in a shallow dish of iodine; the cord will dry up and fall off in a few days.

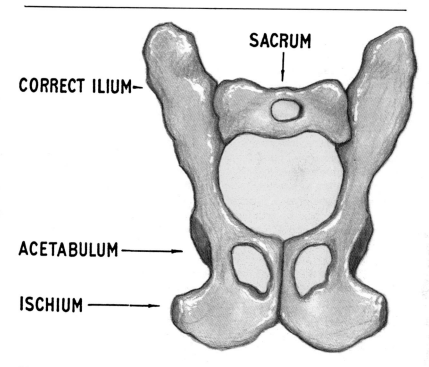

Shape of pelvic entrance in the average female dog, showing adequate aperture through which the whelps have to pass.

The puppies should follow each other at intervals of not more than half an hour. If more time goes past and you are sure there are still pups to come, taking the mother for a brisk walk outside may start labor again. If she is actively straining without producing a puppy, the youngster may be presented backward, a so-called "breech" birth. Careful assistance with a well-lubricated finger to feel for the puppy or to ease it back may help, but never attempt to pull it out by force. This could cause serious damage, so seek the services of an expert—your veterinarian or an experienced breeder.

Even the best planned breeding can bear unexpected problems and complications. Therefore, do not rely solely on textbook knowledge of breeding and genetics. Experienced breeders and veterinarians will generally lend their words of wisdom—take full advantage of their generosity. Mere trial and error is no basis for any responsible breeding program.

If *anything* seems wrong during labor or parturition, waste no time in calling your veterinarian, who will examine the bitch and, if necessary, give her hormones to stimulate the birth of the remaining puppies. You may want his experience in whelping the litter even if all goes well. He will probably prefer to have the puppies born at his hospital rather than getting up in the middle of the night to come

A puppy nurser kit is considered standard equipment by many breeders. These kits are available at your local pet shop.

to your home. The mother would, no doubt, prefer to stay at home; but you can be sure she will get the best of care in a veterinary hospital. If the puppies are born at home, and all goes as it should, watch the mother carefully afterward. Within a day or two of the birth, it is wise to have the veterinarian check her and the pups to ensure that all is well.

Be sure each puppy finds a teat and starts nursing right away, as these first few meals supply colostral antibodies to help him fight disease. As soon as he is dry, hold each puppy to a nipple for a good meal without competition. Then he may join his littermates in the whelping box, out of his mother's way while she continues giving birth. Keep a supply of puppy formula on hand for emergency feedings or later weaning. An alternative formula of evaporated milk, corn syrup, and a little water with egg yolk can be warmed and fed if necessary. A pet nurser kit is also a good thing to have on hand; these are available at local pet shops. A supplementary feeding often helps weak pups (those that may have difficulty nursing) over the hump. Keep track of birth weights and weekly readings thereafter; this will furnish an accurate record of the pups' growth and health, and the information will be valuable to your veterinarian.

RAISING THE PUPPIES

After all the puppies have been born, take the mother outside for a walk and drink of water, and then return her to take care of her brood. She will probably not want to stay away for more than a minute or two for the first few weeks. Be sure to keep water available at all times and feed her milk or broth frequently, as she needs nourishment to produce milk. Encourage her to eat, with her favorite foods, until she seeks them of her own accord. She will soon develop a ravenous appetite and should have at least two large meals a day, with dry food available in addition. Your veterinarian can guide you on the finer points of nutrition as they apply to nursing dams.

Prepare a warm place to put the puppies after they are born to keep them dry and to help them to a good start in life. An electric heating pad, heat lamp or hot water bottle covered with flannel can be placed in the bottom of a cardboard box and near the mother so that she can see her puppies. She will usually allow you to help her care for the youngsters, but don't take them out of her sight. Let her handle things if your interference seems to make her nervous.

Be sure that all the puppies are getting enough to eat. If the mother sits or stands instead of lying still to nurse, the probable cause is scratching from the puppies' nails. You can remedy this by clipping them, as you would the bitch's, with a pet nail clipper. Manicure scissors also do for these tiny claws. Some breeders advise disposing of the smaller or weaker pups in a large litter, as the mother has trouble handling more than six or seven. You can help her out by preparing an extra puppy box or basket furnished with a heating pad and/or heating lamp and some bedding material. Leave half the litter with the mother and the other half in the extra box, changing off at two-hour intervals at first. Later you may exchange them less frequently, leaving them all together except during the day. Try supplementary feedings, too. As soon as their eyes open, at about two weeks, they will lap from a small dish.

WEANING THE PUPPIES

Normally the puppies should be completely weaned at five weeks, although you can start to feed them at three weeks. They will find it easier to lap semi-solid food than to drink milk at first, so mix baby cereal with whole or evaporated milk, warmed to body temperature, and offer it to the puppies in a saucer. Until they learn to lap it, it is best to feed one or two at a time because they are more likely to walk into it than to eat it. Hold the saucer at their chin level, and let them gather around, keeping paws off

Breeding

Excessively long puppy nails can scratch the whelping mother's tummy and teats, making the bitch little inclined to nurse the pups. Specially designed clippers for trimming the nails are available at your local pet shop.

the dish. Cleaning with a damp sponge afterward prevents most of the cereal from sticking to the pups if the mother doesn't clean them up. Once they have gotten the idea, broth or babies' meat soup may be alternated with milk, and you can start them on finely chopped meat. At about four weeks, they will eat four meals a day and soon do without their mother entirely. Start them on canned dog food, or leave dry puppy food with them in a dish for self-feeding. Don't leave the water dish with them all the time; at this age everything is a play toy and they will use it as a wading pool. They can drink all they need if it is offered several times a day, after meals. As the puppies grow up, the mother will go into their "pen" only to nurse them, first sitting up and then standing. To dry up her milk

supply completely, keep the mother away for longer periods; after a few days of part-time nursing she can stay away for even longer periods, and then permanently. The little milk left will be resorbed by her body.

The puppies may be put outside during the day, unless it is too cold or rainy, as soon as their eyes are open. They will benefit from the sunlight. A rubber mat or newspapers underneath will protect them from cold or dampness. As they mature, the pups can be let out for longer intervals, although you must provide them with a shelter at night or in bad weather. By now, cleaning up after the matured youngsters is a man-sized job, so put them out at least during the day and make your task easier. If you enclose them in a run or kennel, remember to clean it *daily*, as various parasites and other infectious organisms may be lurking if the quarters are kept dirty.

You can expect the pups to need at least one worming before they are ready to go to new homes. Before the pups are three weeks old, take a stool sample from each to your veterinarian. The vet can determine, by analyzing the stool, if any of the pups have worms—and if so, what kind of worms are present. If one puppy is infected, then all should be wormed as a preventive measure. Follow the veterinarian's advice; this also applies to vaccinations. You will want to vaccinate the pups at the earliest possible age. This way, the pups destined for new homes will be protected against some of the more debilitating canine diseases.

THE DECISION TO SPAY OR NEUTER

If you decide not to use your male or female for breeding, or if you are obligated to have the animal altered based on an agreement made between you and the seller, make the necessary arrangements with your veterinarian as soon as possible. The surgery involved for both males and females is relatively simple and painless: males will be castrated and females will have their ovaries and uterus removed. In both cases, the operation does not alter their personalities; you will, however, notice that males will be less likely to roam, to get into fights with other male dogs, and to mount objects and people.

Your veterinarian can best determine at what age neutering or spaying should be done. With a young female dog, the operation may be somewhat more involved, and as a result be more costly; however, in the long run you will be glad you made the decision to have this done for your pet. After a night or two at the veterinarian's or an animal hospital, your bitch can be safely returned to your home. Her stitches will heal in a short time, and when they are removed, you will hardly notice her souvenir scar of the routine operation. Once she has been spayed, she no longer will be capable of having a litter of puppies. Pet adoption agencies and other animal welfare organizations can house only so many animals at one time, given the money, space, and other resources they have available. This is why pet owners are urged to have their pets altered, so that puppies resulting from accidental breedings won't end up being put to sleep as so many others have that are lost, stray, unwanted, or abandoned.

Top view of a dog's skeletal structure. The dog is a highly specialized animal.

Dogs and the Law

By Anmarie Barrie, Esq.

This chapter is written merely as a general survey of the laws pertaining to dogs. The laws vary tremendously from jurisdiction to jurisdiction. They also change over time, and are subject to the interpretation of the controlling authorities.

Any reference to a resource material or facility is not an endorsement.

As civilization advances and living conditions become more crowded, laws are created to keep society functioning smoothly. Our lives become more regulated. This includes how we care for our dogs.

Laws dealing with dogs are in effect at all levels of government. Mostly, though, dog law is a local affair. There are many dog laws. They vary from country to country and from city to city. However, there are general rules and guidelines that are common to all dog laws.

BUYING AND SELLING

Most of the law regulating buyers, sellers, and breeders of dogs pertains to dealers. A dealer is a person who buys and sells dogs in the regular course of his business. Therefore, an owner who sells the family pet's puppies at a yard sale is not covered. However, some laws do encompass the occasional seller.

If you regularly sell, keep, or breed more than a certain number of dogs, you may need a kennel or breeder's license. Puppies may or may not be included in this number. Usually diseased dogs, and dogs under a specified age, are forbidden to be sold.

Whether you are the buyer or the seller, put the sales agreement in writing. Until you write it out, you may not realize that you and the other party have different understandings. The agreement should include, but is certainly not limited to, the following:

1. Breed, sex, age, color, quality, and birth date of the dog
2. Names and addresses of

the buyer and the seller

3. Name and address of the breeder

4. Names and registration numbers of the sire and dam (pedigree)

5. Date of the last veterinary exam, the name and address of the veterinarian, and any findings

6. Date and types of vaccinations

7. Behavior (viciousness) and propensities (training) of the dog

8. Any health problems the dog may have

9. Any warranties (guarantees) the seller is making

10. The name of the original owner (if the seller purchased the dog from someone else).

GENERAL GUIDELINES FOR DOG OWNERS

Licenses

Probably wherever you live, a dog needs a license. A license involves a fee and usually has to be renewed periodically. It should be worn by the dog at all times. Puppies under a certain age are exempt from the licensing requirements. A license may cost less for a spayed or neutered dog, an assistance dog, or a dog belonging to an old or disabled person. To find out where to get a license, talk to your pet shop owner, veterinarian, local officials, the animal control or health department, or look in the telephone book.

Licensed and unlicensed dogs may be accorded different treatment under the law. Any unlicensed dog, or a dog running at large without a license tag, may be impounded. Unlicensed dogs that are impounded are destroyed or sold sooner than licensed dogs, because local authorities are unable to trace ownership. Furthermore, some authorities permit the killing of an unlicensed dog, or a licensed dog not wearing its license, at any given time. Yet a dog wearing a license can be killed only if it is attacking a person or livestock.

Dogs and the Law

If your dog is lost or stolen, it will be harder to find if it does not have a license. An owner of an unlicensed dog may be subject to a fine or penalty.

Vaccinations

A current rabies vaccination is a common requirement. Other inoculations, such as a distemper shot, may be necessary as well. Proof of vaccination may be required in order to get a license. Puppies under a certain age are not required to be vaccinated.

Leash Laws

Many areas have leash laws. These laws require a dog to be under the control of its owner at all times. This may involve confinement, that the dog be on a leash, or even muzzled.

No dog should be allowed to roam free. A dog at large could be impounded and disposed of according to regulations. Its owner may be fined and have to pay for the cost of confining the dog. Some communities have special areas where dogs are allowed to run loose.

Other Restrictions

Muzzle laws are becoming more popular, as are laws requiring owners to clean up their dog's solid waste (pooper-scooper laws) if   deposited anywhere off their own property. Many buildings, such as restaurants, apartments, and hotels, and other areas, such as beaches, are strictly off limits to dogs. Owners of assistance dogs are commonly excluded from these laws.

You should also be aware that some municipalities actually prohibit a dog from being left alone in a car. An owner may be violating anti-cruelty laws.

How Many Dogs Allowed?

Many animal lovers have more than one dog. However, some communities restrict the number of dogs allowed per household, and some residencies refuse to permit dogs at all.

These laws are taken quite seriously. If your condominium or apartment lease has a no-pets clause, you can be evicted for harboring a dog. If your residence limits the number of dogs you can keep, exceeding that number can subject you to a daily fine.

If you want to keep more dogs, you may need to apply for a city permit or a kennel license. This may entail extra fees, rules, and inspections.

An owner may be required to dispose of the number of dogs exceeding the allowable limit. Fines and jail sentences can be imposed as well. These enforcement measures can be imposed even if you are caring for someone else's dog only temporarily. Puppies less than a certain age may or may not be exempted.

Lost and Found

If your dog is lost, call any agency you think handles dogs. Include the police, health and animal control departments, and humane societies. Listen to local radio stations and read the local newspapers that list found animals. Visit the police station,

animal shelter, and government offices where lists may be posted. Leave a picture and an accurate description of the dog every place you visit. If at first you are not successful, keep asking around. The dog may show up later.

If you find a dog, attempt to find its owner, or give the dog to the local authorities. If you do not make an effort to return the dog to its owner, you may be liable to the owner for the value of the dog. The law may require you to notify the animal control authorities.

If the dog remains in your possession, check for

identification. The dog may have the name and address of its owner on a tag. Call the owner. If the dog has a license tag, call the agency that issued the tag to get the name of the owner.

Ask local residents if they recognize the dog. Post signs around the area where the dog was found. Put a notice in the paper and notify the local radio station.

Impoundment laws often give animal control officials the authority to pick up, impound,

sell, and/or destroy dogs. However, since a dog is considered the personal property of its owner, a dog cannot be confiscated without notice, and possibly a hearing.

An owner's property rights may be lost, though, under certain conditions. Any unlicensed dog, or a dog running at large without a vaccination tag, or running at large without a license tag may be impounded without first notifying its owner.

Dogs running around loose are

typical pound inhabitants. injured, abandoned, and vicious dogs also end up at the pound. A dog that has bitten a person, caused damage, or been declared a nuisance can be taken from its owner and impounded. An owner who has his dog in his possession, though, is entitled to be notified before the dog is seized. An owner must usually be notified again before the dog is destroyed.

A pound is required to keep the dog for a prescribed period of time before it can take action. If the owner can be identified, he must be notified. To reclaim the dog, an owner may have to have the dog licensed, vaccinated, pay a fine, and pay a charge for every day that the dog is kept. If the owner does not claim the dog, it can be sold, offered for adoption, or killed in a humane manner. The law may allow a dog to be given to an assistance dog agency or a research facility.

Dog laws may be enforced by any number of agencies. These include the police, a humane society, an animal control center, or a health department. No matter which organization is responsible for enforcing the law, all of them must respect the legal rights of an owner.

Burial

Contact your local animal control authority for information on how to dispose of your dog's remains. You may not be permitted to bury the dog on your own property. You may have to bring the dog's body to a pet cemetery. The wisest thing to do is to have your vet handle the burial. Some towns will dispose of the dog for a fee.

DOGS AS PROPERTY

A dog is personal property. This fact has a lot of legal implications, because an owner of property has legally enforceable rights. The law prohibits a person from injuring, taking, or destroying the property of another. So an owner who has a property interest in his dog is entitled to compensation if his dog is killed, stolen, or injured.

Damages typically include actual out-of-pocket expenses. But other criteria may have some bearing as well. For example, consider the market value and age of the dog. Its type, traits, pedigree, and purchase price are all legitimate concerns. The feelings of the owner will probably not be considered in a damage award. Other considerations include registration, breeding value, value as a watchdog, and if the dog is expecting a litter.

For an owner to enforce his rights as an owner of property, the dog may need to be licensed. An owner of an unlicensed dog may not be afforded any protection under the law. An owner of a puppy that does not yet require a license should still benefit from the property laws concerning dogs.

Since a dog is not a person, it cannot be a beneficiary of a will. It cannot inherit money or other property. If you want your dog to be cared for after your death, you must designate a new owner for the dog in your will. It is wise to leave money to the new owner to care for your dog. Be sure to consider medical expenses—as your dog gets older, its veterinary bills will increase.

A dog may be contested property in a divorce proceeding. A court will determine custody and visitation rights.

Property cannot be taken from an owner without due process of the law. This means that the dog owner must have notice, and possibly be given a hearing before his property is taken or destroyed. Therefore, before a dog can be impounded, killed, or offered for adoption, its owner must be given adequate notice. The amount of time considered "adequate notice" varies from place to place and may depend on whether or not the dog is licensed.

Who is Responsible for the Dog?

An owner is legally responsible for controlling his dog. However, the definition of an owner may be broad enough to include the legal owner, as well as anyone who cares for, harbors, or has custody of the dog. So someone besides the owner, or more than one person, may be liable for the actions of the dog.

A dog owner may be a minor. In such a situation, the youngster's parents or legal guardian may be responsible for any injury or damage caused by the dog. Under certain circumstances, a landlord may be responsible. The landlord must have known that a tenant's dog was dangerous, have had

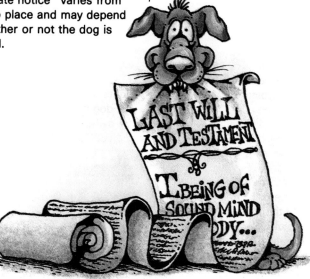

the power to remove the dog, but did nothing about it.

A veterinarian and his staff members may be injured by a dog during the course of its treatment. The dog owner is probably not responsible because these people know and accept the risk of injury. Of course, an owner cannot conceal the fact that his dog is dangerous. A doctor has insurance to cover these mishaps.

Liability for Damage and Injury

Typically, an owner is legally liable for any personal injury or property damage (including killing livestock) caused by his pet. Depending upon the circumstances, an owner may be fined or jailed as well.

An owner may have to pay medical expenses. This can include costs for doctors, hospitals, medications, physical therapy, and counselling. A victim may also be entitled to compensation for loss of earnings if he was out of work due to his injury. The time off may involve both treatment and recuperation.

Some victims of dog attacks are awarded compensation for pain and suffering. The amount of the award can vary tremendously depending on the circumstances because it is difficult to calculate the cost specifically. Sometimes a spouse or close relative can receive compensation as well. The theory is loss of service of the injured person. Loss of service is not limited to economics; it may also include loss of companionship.

If the fault on the part of the owner is particularly shocking or reckless, an award may be doubled or even tripled. Additionally, the victim may be entitled to punitive damages. This recovery punishes the owner's poor conduct by making him pay even more than the amount considered adequate compensation to the victim. The financial status of the owner can be taken into account when establishing a punitive damage award.

Also, the owner will have to take measures designed to prevent further detriment. In serious cases, this could mean destruction of the dog. Since any dog can cause injury or damage under the right circumstances, a prudent owner will take precautionary measures designed to prevent his dog from causing harm.

There are several legal theories under which dog owners may be found liable for their dog's acts. Some of the

theories are strict liability, common law rules, negligence, and nuisance. Strict liability means that the owner is responsible for the dog's actions even though the owner is not at fault in any way. Common law doctrines are defined in court decisions. They are not codified in statutes. An owner is negligent if he does not exercise reasonable and ordinary care in controlling his dog. A dog is a nuisance if it unreasonably and substantially offends or inconveniences a person.

Often there is an on-duty exemption for trained police or military dogs. The police or government may be immune from liability if the injury occurred because the dog was

Dogs and the Law

provoked or while it was working.

Vicious Dogs

Once a dog has bitten or exhibited menacing behavior, it may be officially declared a vicious dog. Dogs that have been trained to attack or fight may also be considered vicious. A few dog breeds are believed to be inherently dangerous.

Owners of such vicious dogs may be required to take further measures to control their dogs. The dogs may have to be securely confined at all times, on a leash and muzzled when in public, and have a special vicious dog license. The dog may have to be tattooed. The owner may be required to have liability insurance for the dog. Signs may be necessary to warn the public that a vicious dog is in residence. A bond may have to be posted with the municipality to cover any potential injury or damage. Some cities ban vicious dogs.

An owner who fails to comply with the law may be fined or jailed. He may also be liable for double or triple the amount of damage caused by the dog. The dog may be impounded and killed.

Preventing Injury

If you are a dog owner or keeper, the best way to avoid liability is to prevent injury. Adhere to a few common sense rules to keep risk of harm to a minimum.

No matter how small, old or timid the dog is, it can hurt someone, damage property, or be a nuisance. Any dog may bite or scratch if it is threatened, or if it is protecting its owner, its puppies, or its food. A dog racing around a corner or barking unexpectedly may startle an unsuspecting person and result in injury.

Therefore, keep your dog securely contained in the house or yard. Be sure it cannot escape to scare or otherwise get in the way of strangers. Post warning signs that alert passers-by that a dog is present. Never let your dog off its leash to run at large. The owner must be in control at all times.

Lastly, keep the dog's license and vaccinations up-to-date. If your dog does manage to get free, its return will be more expedient if it is properly identified. The less time out of your care, the less time the dog has to cause trouble. Should the dog bite someone, the dog will not need to be quarantined if its rabies vaccine is current.

Dogs and the Law

Insurance

The cost of the potential damage and injury inflicted by a dog can be enormous. A wise owner will check to see that his homeowner's or renter's policy covers his dog. A dog that has a menacing behavior should have its own insurance coverage. Dangerous and vicious dogs may be obligated by law to have liability insurance.

A typical homeowner's or renter's insurance plan covers any damage caused by the policy holder's negligence. This coverage often extends to incidents that take place away from the owner's property, even if a vehicle is involved. If policy does not extend to vehicular events, look to your auto insurance plan. Some insurance companies refuse to issue a policy altogether if a vicious dog lives in the home.

Often a plan limits its coverage to the first instance of harm caused by a dog. After that, the owner must pay out of his own pocket. Other companies exclude certain types of dog-related harm from their coverage. This is why it is important to read your policy carefully. If you do not understand the terms, call your agent for an explanation. It is important to know your liability before an accident occurs.

If your home and auto insurance do not extend to dog-related injuries, or you think the coverage is not broad enough, buy insurance for your pet. Take out insurance that will protect you and the dog while at home and/or away.

Your dog may become ill or injured. Get coverage that will pay for its medical expenses. Some insurance firms offer pet health insurance. These policies may pay for medications, doctors' bills, and hospital fees.

Handling a Controversy

A dog can be dangerous, or it can be just a nuisance. Either way, if you have a dog like this in your neighborhood, or if it is your dog, you may be involved in a dispute. Your dog may have caused injury or damage, or your dog may have been the victim. Either way, you should be prepared to handle the controversy in a responsible and legally acceptable manner.

A dog may not be dangerous, but it can be a nuisance. Some irksome antics include digging up a yard, chasing a car, scattering garbage across the lawn, ravaging a prized garden, barking incessantly, roaming the neighborhood, and frightening people.

If you are the property owner, the first thing to do is to talk to the owner of the dog. Use a reasonable and friendly approach—*avoid animosity*. Offer your neighbor some advice as to how to stop the dog's bad habits. Suggest obedience school or calling the local humane society for some tips. If the dog's poor behavior stops, call on your neighbor again to thank him for taking the necessary measures.

If you happen to be the owner of the dog wreaking havoc, be understanding, not hostile. After all, you are responsible for keeping your dog from annoying your neighbors. Your neighbor has probably had several encounters with your dog before he came to talk to you. Take the proper measures to stop the

dog's poor behavior. After a few days, visit your neighbor to be sure the problem has been solved.

If talking to your neighbor is a dead-end, try mediation. This method of settling disputes outside of a courtroom involves the imposition of a neutral third party. This individual acts as a link between the disputing parties to keep the lines of communication open. A mediator does not choose sides, he merely identifies problems and suggests compromises. Once the differences are settled, define the terms in a writing signed by both parties.

There may be a reason that you do not want to talk to your neighbor, or talking to him proves disastrous, or maybe you just do not know who owns the troublesome dog. Call your police, animal control department, health or public safety authorities. The people responsible for controlling dogs can call or visit the dog owner, or even issue a citation.

Look up all the pertinent local law, such as ordinances dealing with noise, vicious dogs, leash laws, nuisances, dogs running at large, personal injury, property damage, or the number of dogs allowed per household, and have it enforced. Enlist the aid of other neighbors who are annoyed. And, most importantly, be persistent.

You may be compelled to go to court. If so, familiarize yourself with the law so that you can make sure your complaint meets all the required elements. Good preparation is vital to presenting a sound argument. Be brief and articulate, not boring. Present your case in an organized manner. You may be allowed to present witnesses, and to utilize documents, police reports, hospital records, medical bills, and photographs. Avoid confusion or repetition. But most importantly, always be respectful to both the judge and your adversary.

CRUELTY

In most modern societies, cruelty against dogs is forbidden. Inhumane treatment may include intentional abuse, neglect, theft, abandonment, and dog fighting. Cropping ears and tails without using anesthesia, leaving a dog which was hit by your car, confining a dog in a parked car, and poor conditions in a shelter may all be considered cruelty. In Great Britain, ear cropping is expressly prohibited. It is lawful, though, to kill a dog in the act of injuring a person or damaging property. Using dogs for scientific research is usually not punishable by law, even though it is distasteful.

If you suspect improper behavior, first talk to the owner. If the maltreatment does not cease, report the abuse to the humane society, the police, a local dog society, or anyone else you think has the right to take action. It is best to have the complaint in writing. Keep a copy for yourself.

Except in the case of an emergency, the dog owner is entitled to notice before his dog can be taken away. A mistreated dog is seized by the authorities and impounded. If the cruelty is particularly outrageous, the abuser may be subject to a fine or a jail sentence.

TRAVEL

It is a common sight to see a

dog owner traveling with his pet. In fact, many owners refuse to go anywhere without their dog. However, most owners do not realize that traveling is stressful for their pet. So if you are not going to leave your dog at home, at least make the trip as comfortable as possible.

Restrictions regarding pet travel are constantly changing due to health and international situations. Therefore, call the appropriate agricultural department, embassy, or consulate before departing. Most countries require a recent certificate of health. Vaccinations may be necessary.

Of course, your dog should be properly identified. A tag with the dog's name, and your name, address, and phone number should be attached to the dog at all times.

Each container should be plainly marked, labeled, or tagged on the outside with the names and addresses of the shipper and the consignee. An accurate invoice statement specifying the number of each species contained in the shipment must also be included.

Since the hours of service and the availability of inspectors vary from port to port, check with your anticipated port of arrival prior to importation. This will reduce the possibility of unnecessary delay.

An airline may refuse to transport an animal unless specific criteria are met. Common restrictions include that the dog must be at least eight weeks old; certified as healthy; secured in a carrier; and adequately identified.

A dog traveling on an airline must be contained in a shipping crate. The crate should be sturdy and well ventilated. It should be large enough to allow your pet to stand, turn around, and lie down comfortably. The carrier should be marked "*Live Animals*" and "*This End Up.*" Your name, address, and phone number, the dog's name, and the destination should be on the crate.

LANDLORDS AND DOGS

Many landlords prefer not to rent to dog owners. A dog can disturb other tenants if it is noisy, messy, or smelly. Under the right circumstances, any dog can destroy property or injure a person. A landlord can experience a lot of aggravation and expense. Violation of an existing no-pets clause may be a sufficient cause for eviction or a penalty.

A no-dogs policy may be negotiable. An exception may be made if the prospective tenant can assure the landlord that the dog will not be a problem. But how do you convince the landlord?

There are several things that can be done. Introduce the dog to the landlord. The landlord can see for himself that the dog is well groomed and well mannered. An untrained puppy is not as desirable as a mature, adult dog. A spayed or neutered dog will probably get bonus points. Bring along written references from previous landlords and neighbors saying that the dog has not been a problem and is well liked.

Special provisions can be negotiated in private leases that are fair to both sides. Dog owners are still responsible for damage and injury caused by their dogs.

Index

Abdomen, cysts in, 137;
swelling of, 129
Aerobic activity, 78–79
Afterbirth, eating of, 166
Aggressiveness, 105–109
Aging process, 136–137
American Kennel Club,
47
Amniotic membrane, 166
Anatomy, digestive
system, 59; organs of
dog, 42
Artificial respiration, 125
Barking, 101–104
Bed, dog, 69, 70–71
Bitch, whelping, 163–165
Biting, law regarding, 182
Black widow spider, 121
"Breech" birth, 167
Breed club, national, 37
Breeder's contract, 153
Breeding, license and,
172
Brown dog tick, 133
Bufo marinus, 122
Burial, 177
Calculus, 147
Caloric requirements, 68
Canine hepatitis, 129
Car accidents, 126
Caries, dental, 138
Castration, 42, 170
Check-ups, veterinary, 51
Chewing need, 138–140
Chew toys, 114
Children, 44, 52
Cleanliness, 77
Colostral antibodies, 168
Commercial dog foods,
60
Confinement, 72, 73, 78–
79
Consistency, in training,
50, 91, 94
Controversies, handling,
184–185
Crate, dog, 69, 72–74; for
traveling, 189

Cruelty, laws pertaining
to, 187
Death, disposal of
remains, 177
Debarking, 101
Deer fly, 133
Deer tick, 132
Destructive behavior, 71,
90, 109, 143
Distemper, 129, 139
Divorce, and dogs, 179
Dog house, 69, 74–76
Dogs, damages accrued
or assigned, 178–179
Dominance, 105
Duke, Dr. Andrew, 147
Dumbbell, 97
Ear mites, 127–128
Elimination on command,
87
Elizabethan collars, 126
Estrus, 155–157
Evolution of dog, 35
Feeding, chart, 68;
commercial dog foods
and, 60; routine and,
65
Female, whelping, 163–
165
Fertilization, 155
Fetching, 82
First aid kits, 112;
supplies, 113
Flaws, not to breed to, 40
Fleas, 133–135; life cycle
of, 135; tapeworm and,
133
Flossing, for dental
hygiene, 145–146
Foxglove, 55
Frisbee® Flying Discs, 80
Gestation, 163
Giant toad, 122
Gumabone®, as chew
product, 51; as
exercise tool, 118; as
therapeutic device,

147, 150, 151, 152;
polyurethane balls, 85
Gumadisc®, 82
Handling, 52
Health certificates, 52
Heartworm, 133, 134–
135; life cycle of, 136
"Heat," bitch's, 155–157
Holding a dog, 128
Hookworms, 135
Housebreaking, 87–91
Human remedies, 112
Illness, signs of, 127–
128; symptoms of, 113
Impregnation, multiple,
163
Inhalation pneumonia,
119
Inoculations, 52, 128
Insect bites, 128
Insurance, for the dog,
182, 184
Intermediate host, 133
"Junk food", 65
Kennel Club of Great
Britain, 47
Kennel cough, 132
Kennels, 76
Kidneys, inflammation of,
129
Knee joint, 79
Lactrodectus mactans,
121
Landlords, 189
Larkspur, 127
Leases, dogs and, 189
Leash laws, 174
Legal responsibilities,
179–182
Leptospirosis, 129
License, 48; breeding
and, 172; laws
regarding, 173
Life span, 42
Lily-of-the valley, 120
Loss of hair, and
pregnancy, 165

Lost dogs, 175–177
Lyme Disease, 132
Medicine, administration, 123; liquid and pill, 123
Mendelian expectation chart, 164
Mice, 131
Micro filaria, 1365
Mitosis, 154
Mosquito bites, 136
Muzzle, emergency, 122–123, 126; laws, 174
Neighbors, 185
Neutering, 153
Newspapers, used for punishment, 89
New York Academy of Dog Training, 95
Nightshade, 127
Nurser, puppy, 168
Nursing dams, feeding and, 168
Nylabone®, as chew product, 51; as exercise tool, 118; as pacifier, 71, 117; as therapeutic device, 142, 143; as toy, 111; nylon balls, 85
Nylafloss®, for dental hygiene, 145, 146
Nylon chews, 142–143
Nylon discs, 81
Nylon toys, 114–118
Obedience trial equipment, 97
Old dogs, 136–137; vitamins and, 137
Ovaries, removed, 170
Overfeeding, 67
Ovulation, 154
Pack instincts, 105
Pads, foot, injury to, 113
Paper training, 88, 89
Parainfluenza, 132
Parasites, control of, 77; external, 133; internal, 135
Parvovirus, 131–132
Pedigree papers, 46, 47, 48

Pelvic entrance, 167
Penis, 161
Periodontal disease, 146–147
Perpetual whelping chart, 159
Planned departures, 110–111
Plaque, 147
Poisoning, 118–119; 120–121
Pokeweed, 55
Polyurethane toys, 82, 118
Pooch Pacifiers®, 117, 143
Pooper-scooper laws, 174
Pregnancy, and appetite, 164; and exercise, 164; and hair loss, 165
Punishment, 95, 102–103; delayed, 89
Rabies, 129–131
Rats, 130
Rawhide, 140–142, 149
Registration papers, 46, 48
Restraining a dog, 128
Restrictions regarding dogs, 189
Road accidents, 124
Roundworms, 135
Routine, in feeding, 65; in training, 51
Running away, 95
Sacrum, 167
Selection, adult or pup, 43–44; male or female, 42–43
Self-feeding, 62
Selling litters, 158
Sexual urges, male's, 156
Shock, signs of, 124
Show-quality, 153
Socialization, 91
Spaying, 42, 153, 154
"Speak," barking and, 101, 102
Stable fly, 132
Stifle joint, 79

Stud dog, 158–159
Supplements, food, 62; vitamin and mineral, 63, 164
Surrogate mothers, 58
Symptoms of illness, 113
Tapeworm, 133, 135; cycle of, 137
Tartar, 138
Temperature, as sign of labor, 165; bodily, 113
Territory, male's, 156
Ticks, 132, 133
Tooth care, professional, 152
Toys, 80; hard rubber, 114; nylon, 114–118
Training, 91–101; "Come", 98; "Down", 99–100; "Heel", 98; "Sit", 96; "Stay", 96–97
Training collars, 93
Travel, 122; restrictions regarding dogs, 188
Tug toys, 84
Umbilical cord, 166
Umbilical hernia, 166
United Kennel Club, 47
Uterus, before mating, 162; with whelps, 163
Vaccination, 162; for pups, 170; laws regarding, 173
Veterinary care, 112
Veterinary check-ups, 51
Vicious dogs, laws regarding, 181
Vitamins, older dogs and, 137
Vomiting, induced, 119
Water bucket approach, 103
Water hemlock, 120
Weaning, 169–170
Whelping, 158, 166–168; bitch and, 163–165; box, 156, 165; chart, 159
Whipworms, 135
Wills and dog, 189
Worming, for pups, 170
Yew, 55

Required Reading

The Atlas of Dog Breeds of the World By Bonnie Wilcox, DVM, & Chris Walkowicz (H-1091)
Traces the history and highlights the characteristics, appearance and function of every recognized dog breed in the world. 409 different breeds receive full-color treatment and individual study. Hundreds of breeds in addition to those recognized by the American Kennel Club and the Kennel Club of Great Britain are included—the dogs of the world complete! The ultimate reference work, comprehensive coverage, intelligent and delightful discussions. The perfect gift book. *Hard cover, 9" × 12", 912 pages, 1,106 color photos. ISBN 0-86622-930-2*

Dog Training By Lew Burke (H-962)
The elements of dog training are easy to grasp and apply. The author uses the psychological makeup of dogs to his advantage by making them want to be what they should be—substituting the family for the pack. *Hard cover, 5½" × 8", 255 pages, 64 black and white photos, 23 color photos. ISBN 0-87666-656-X*

The Complete Dog Buyer's Guide By Dr. William Bruette & Kerry V. Donnelly (H-989)
Plots the advances in veterinary care and genetics of the last fifty years by incorporating descriptions of the breeds as they are today. Many of the photos illustrate Best In Show winners and top and historical dogs. Individual complete sections on breeding, selection, caring, etc. *Hard cover, 5½" × 8", 608 pages. Illustrated. ISBN 0-86622-026-7*

The Mini Atlas of Dog Breeds By Andrew De Prisco & James B. Johnson (H-1106)
An identification handbook giving a concise and thorough look at over 400 of the world's dog breeds. The authors' enthusiastic and knowledgeable approach brings to life instantly man's oldest friend and companion. A flowing and witty text, further enlivened by 500 full-color photos, successfully maps out the world of dogs; an easy-reference format pinpoints each breed's development, portrait, registry, and pet attributes. The volume is captioned with specially designed symbols. *Hard cover, 5½" × 8½", 544 pages, nearly 700 color photos. ISBN 0-86622-091-7*

Dog Owner's Encyclopedia of Veterinary Medicine By Allan H. Hart, B.V.Sc. (H-934)
Written by a vet who feels that most dog owners should recognize the symptoms and understand the cures of most diseases of dogs so they can properly communicate with their veterinarian. This book is a necessity for every dog owner, especially those who have more than one dog. *Hard cover, 5½" × 8", 186 pages, 86 black and white photos. ISBN 0-87666-287-4*

Dog Breeding for Professionals By Dr. Herbert Richards (H-969)
For dog owners who need and actively seek good advice about how to go about breeding their dogs whether for profit or purely because of their attachment to animals. *Please note* that the breeding photography is sexually explicit and some readers may find it offensive. *Hard cover, 5½" × 8", 224 pages, 105 black and white photos, 62 color photos. ISBN 0-87666-659-4*

Dogs and the Law By Anmarie Barrie, Esq. (DS-130)
A practical and reliable survey of laws pertaining to our dogs. Advice concerning liability, licenses, impoundment, vehicles, insurance, wills, vaccinations and many other useful and often entertaining topics. Full color cartoon illustrations add a delightful twist. *Hard cover, 6" × 9", 160 pages, over 55 color illustrations, appendices, charts. ISBN 0-86622-088-7*